VOICE LESSONS

Understanding the Writer's Tools

by Nancy Dean

REVISED EDITION

MAUPIN HOUSE BY
CAPSTONE PROFESSIONAL
a capstone imprint

Voice Lessons Revised Edition
Understanding the Writer's Tools

By Nancy Dean

Cover Design and Cover Artwork: Charmaine Whitman and Lisa King
Interior Design: Lisa King
Design Element: Shutterstock: Ekkasit Rakrotchit

Library of Congress Cataloging-in-Publication Data
Names: Dean, Nancy, 1945– author.
Title: Voice lessons : understanding the writer's tools / by Nancy Dean.
Description: Revised edition. | North Mankato, Minnesota : Capstone Press,
    2019. | Series: Maupin House | Includes bibliographical references.
Identifiers: LCCN 2018004941 (print) | LCCN 2018005725 (ebook) |
    ISBN 9781496609748 (eBook PDF) | ISBN 9781496609755 (reflowable epub) |
    ISBN 9781496609731 (pbk.)
Subjects: LCSH: English language—Composition and exercises—Study and
    teaching (Secondary)
Classification: LCC LB1631 (ebook) | LCC LB1631 .D295 2018 (print) |
    DDC 808/.0420712—dc23
LC record available at https://lccn.loc.gov/2018004941

Maupin House publishes professional resources for K–12 educators. Contact us for
tailored, in-school training or to schedule an author for a workshop or conference.
Visit www.capstonepd.com for free lesson plan downloads.

Maupin House Publishing, Inc. by Capstone Professional
1710 Roe Crest Drive
North Mankato, MN 56003
www.capstonepd.com
888-262-6135
info@capstonepd.com

Dedication

For Paul and Kerry

Seth and Keren

Acknowledgments

A heartfelt thanks to Eric Lemstrom, extraordinary teacher and fellow logophile, for his careful reading of the manuscript and his perceptive, student-centered suggestions. The lessons of this book are immeasurably enhanced by his contributions.

To Chris Morris—teacher, principal, colleague, and friend—acknowledgment is paltry thanks. Her clear and persistent voice in support of students and teachers has been an inspiration. Her personal commitment to the many lives she has touched is profound. She is always and truly an educator. She is always and truly a treasured friend.

To the teachers who have found *Voice Lessons* useful over the years: Thank you for sharing your experiences and expertise with me.

To Tom, who *still* edits my work, makes me coffee, and lives his life with full conviction.

Table of Contents

To the Teacher:
Introduction to the Revised Edition

✿ *Voice Lessons* was published in the year 2000. The original book offered short excerpts from essays, fiction, poetry, and drama, with a focused look at the elements of voice. In the revised edition of *Voice Lessons*, I have made some changes. I have added a section on figurative language, a needed addition to the study of voice. I have included more nonfiction text to help students see that nonfiction can be as graceful and engaging as fiction, and I have developed lessons on longer works to integrate the elements of voice and help students understand how they work together. In this revised edition, students receive more support for deep analysis of complex, meaningful text. However, the basic structure of the lessons remains the same, as does the purpose.

Central to *Voice Lessons* is the conviction that the ability to comprehend the nuances of written thought supports the power to write with skill and grace. The activities of *Voice Lessons* are designed to help students understand and appreciate the power of language. The book gives students practice in reading difficult text with patience, determination, and understanding. In consequence, they learn that writing is not something that just happens. Great writing is studied, crafted, and deliberate. Students learn to recognize the tools that all good writers use to craft their work, and they practice using those tools to control and express their own thoughts. Finally (and most important), the lessons' intent is to teach students to love reading and writing, to enjoy mental challenge, and to express their individual voices with clarity and vision.

Structurally, *Voice Lessons* is a collection of 100 classroom lessons treating the six principal elements of voice: diction, detail, figurative language (added to this revised edition of *Voice Lessons*), imagery, syntax, and tone. Each lesson has

- **a quotation** from complex and critically acclaimed fiction, nonfiction, speeches, drama, or poetry;
- **two discussion questions** that guide the analysis of the quotation, aimed at a specific element of voice; and
- **an application exercise** that incorporates newfound knowledge into practice, asking students to model the element of voice featured in the quotation.

The first section of the book contains lessons based on short quotations. Each quotation illustrates a particular element of voice. There are five lessons each for diction, detail, imagery, syntax, and tone. To address a variety of figures of speech, I have included 10 lessons for figurative language. Please note that the boldface words in all of the diction lessons indicate the words I emphasize in the lessons. Boldface does not appear in the original text. Some selections also include definitions of uncommon or archaic words.

The second section of the book contains lessons based on longer pieces of text, designed to help students examine the elements of voice in sustained writing. The longer works include

- "A Dill Pickle," *Bliss and Other Stories,* by Katherine Mansfield (short story);

- "Of Studies," *The Essays or Counsels, Civil and Moral,* by Sir Francis Bacon (essay);
- "The Death of the Hired Man," *North of Boston,* by Robert Frost (poem);
- A section from Remarks at Amherst College by President John F. Kennedy (speech); and
- Pivotal scenes from *Hamlet* by William Shakespeare (drama).

The intent of this section is to show students how the elements of voice work together. Each of the five longer texts (reproduced for your convenience) is followed by two lessons on each element of voice and a culminating lesson that asks students to write an original work of their own, putting what they have learned into personal practice.

Voice Lessons assumes a passable vocabulary and basic knowledge of sentence structure and grammar. However, to help guide students, I often include some word definitions and explanations of context to facilitate comprehension. In terms of sentence structure and grammar, students should be able to identify simple, compound, complex, and compound-complex sentences. In addition, they should understand the difference between independent and subordinate clauses and have a basic knowledge of punctuation, including dashes and semicolons. If students do not have these fundamentals, you might want to review simple sentence structure and punctuation rules. Sophisticated knowledge of parts of speech is not necessary, and extensive grammar instruction will be more distracting than helpful.

Voice Lessons is a teacher resource guide designed to supplement the regular English curriculum. I recommend using the lessons to stimulate discussion and engender interest in the critical reading of text, the understanding of voice, and the development of students' personal voices. The longer text might also be useful as mini-units to teach close reading, rhetoric, and critical analysis.

You have permission to make copies of the lessons for classroom use. Having copies of the lessons enables students to underline or highlight important parts of the quotations and to take notes on the questions, activities that keep students attentive and engaged.

Lessons usually take 15 to 20 minutes, although some questions and exercises may take longer, and you will need more time for students to read the longer works critically and carefully. To hold students accountable for *Voice Lessons*, I suggest they take notes on the discussion questions and share the application exercises in pairs or small groups. You may want to collect written work after every few lessons. Since much of the work is oral, you can simply skim the written work to ensure students are attentive and practicing. My intent with this book is to give teachers a practical classroom resource that promotes student learning without increasing teacher workload!

I have included my thoughts for answering the discussion questions in the "Discussion Suggestions" sections that accompany the lessons. These are suggestions only and by no means exhaust possible responses to the text, questions, and activities. Undoubtedly, there are many other answers equally valid and more insightful. My objective is to spark discussion and encourage thought. I fully acknowledge and recognize you, the classroom teacher, as the expert. I honor your ideas, your insights, and your dedication.

Although the activities of *Voice Lessons* have proven to be useful in preparing students for Advanced Placement and International Baccalaureate examinations, this book is not a test-preparation book. My goal is to provide rich and challenging reading and writing experiences for *all* students. My hope is that *Voice Lessons* will help students understand and appreciate the power of language, the importance of voice, and the application of voice studies to their personal reading and writing.

I wish you well in your work. We have the opportunity to shape students' voices. That is a gift and a responsibility.

—*Nancy Dean*

To the Student

Children learn to analyze voice when they are young: *She really means it this time*, they whisper, conspirators in the intrigue of family limits. *Did you hear what Dad* didn't *say?* they knowingly observe, well aware of implications. They analyze; they respond. Voice becomes central to communication. So it is. Voice, the color and texture of communication, stamps expression with the indelible mark of personality. It is the expression of who we are: the pitch and timbre of verbalization. Voice is the fingerprint of a person's language.

During my 40-plus years of experience in English education, I have become increasingly aware of the complexity and importance of voice in reading and writing. Understanding voice gives us an appreciation for the richness of language and a deeper understanding of written communication. Through voice we come to know authors and ideas; by exploring voice, we learn to wield language. The aim of *Voice Lessons* is for you to understand how writers express voice and how you can develop a personal voice in your own writing. To do so, you must first learn to recognize voice and analyze its elements.

Voice Lessons focuses on six elements of voice, tools of the writer: diction, detail, figurative language, imagery, syntax, and tone.

- **Diction** (word choice) is the foundation of voice and contributes to all of its elements.
- **Detail** (facts, observations, and incidents) develops a topic, shaping and enriching voice.
- **Figurative language** (the use of nonliteral language) conveys precision and complexity to the reader.
- **Imagery** (verbal representation of sense experience) brings the immediacy of sensory experience to writing and gives voice a distinctive quality.
- **Syntax** (grammatical sentence structure) controls verbal pacing and focus.
- **Tone** (expression of attitude) gives voice its distinctive personality.

A brief discussion of each element follows.

Diction refers to the author's choice of words. Words are the writer's basic tools: Words create the color and texture of the written work. They both reflect and determine the level of formality; they shape the reader's perceptions. When studying serious literature, do not skip over words you do not know. That is tantamount to wearing earplugs to attend a concert. To understand voice, you must both "hear" the words and "feel" their effects. Diction reflects the writer's vision and steers the reader's thought.

Effective voice is shaped by words that are clear, concrete, and exact. Skilled writers eschew words like *pretty*, *very*, *nice*, and *bad*. Instead they search for words that evoke a specific effect. A coat isn't *torn*; it is *tattered*. The antagonist does not *want* revenge; he *thirsts for* revenge. A door does not *shut*; it *thuds*. Specific diction brings the reader into the scene, enabling full participation in the writer's world.

Diction depends on topic, purpose, and occasion. The topic often determines the specificity and sophistication of diction. For example, articles on global warming will include specific, scientific diction—words such as *mitigation, acidification,* and *emissions*. But even nonscientific topics have their own specialized vocabulary: sports, video games, and fashion, for example. The writer's job is to use this specialized vocabulary purposefully and sparingly.

The writer's purpose—whether to convince, entertain, amuse, inform, or implore—also determines diction. Words chosen to impart a particular effect on the reader reflect and sustain the writer's purpose. For example, if an author's purpose is to inform, the reader should expect straightforward diction. On the other hand, if the author's purpose is to entertain, the reader will likely encounter words used in ironic, playful, or unexpected ways.

In addition, diction depends on the occasion. As with clothes, level of formality influences appropriate choices. Formal diction is largely reserved for scholarly writing and serious prose or poetry. Informal diction is the norm in expository essays, newspaper editorials, and works of fiction. Colloquial diction and slang borrow from informal speech and are typically used to create a mood or capture a particular historic or regional dialect. Appropriateness of diction is determined by the norms of society.

When studying diction, you need to understand both connotation (the meaning suggested by a word) and denotation (literal meaning). When a writer calls a character *slender*, the word evokes a different feeling from calling the character *gaunt*. A word's power to produce a strong reaction in the reader lies mainly in its connotative meaning.

Finally, diction can impart freshness and originality to writing. Words used in surprising or unusual ways make us rethink what is known and reexamine meaning. Skilled writers often opt for complexity rather than simplicity, for multiple rather than singular meanings of words. Thus diction, the foundation of voice, shapes your thinking and guides your understanding of the author's idiosyncratic expression of thought: the writer's voice.

Detail includes facts, observations, reasons, and incidents used to develop a thesis or theme and impart voice. Specific details refer to fewer things than general descriptions, thereby creating a precise mental picture. Detail brings life and color to description, focusing the reader's attention and bringing the reader into the scene. Because detail encourages readers to participate in the text, use of detail influences readers' views of the topic, the setting, the narrator, and the author. Detail shapes the reader's attitude by focusing attention: the more specific the detail, the greater the focus on the object or ideas described.

Detail makes an abstraction concrete, particular, and unmistakable, giving the abstraction form. For example, when Macaulay describes Samuel Johnson's table manners in *Life of Samuel Johnson*, the scene comes alive through Johnson's swollen veins and sweaty forehead. By directing your attention to particulars, detail connects abstraction to your lives: to specifics you can imagine, have participated in, or understand vicariously. Detail focuses description and prepares you to join the action. As a result, you can respond with conviction to the impact of the writer's voice.

Detail can also state by understatement, by a *lack* of detail. The absence of specific details, for example, may be in sharp contrast to the intensity of a character's pain. In this case, elaborate, descriptive detail could turn the pain into sentimentality. Good writers choose detail with care, selecting those details that add meaning and avoiding those that trivialize or detract.

Figurative language is language that is not used in a literal way. It's a way of saying one thing and signifying more. Writers use figurative language because it's a rich, strong, and vivid way to express meaning. We are able to say much more in fewer words. When Robert Burns says, *My love is like a red, red rose,* he is saying many things: His love is beautiful, soft, and fragrant. The rose is red, the color of passion and love. This adds another dimension. The rose also has thorns, which says that there's a potential danger in loving her. She may hurt him. By comparing his love to a red rose, the poet is able to compress many ideas into a single line.

Figurative language can be overdone. When a figure of speech is overused, it loses its freshness and originality and becomes a cliché. Here are some examples of figures of speech that have become clichés:

- I'm all ears.
- She was bent out of shape.
- dead as a doornail
- green-eyed monster
- My hands are tied.

There are many more. These overused figures of speech no longer get the reader's attention. As you sharpen your skills with figurative language, search for figures of speech that you haven't heard a million times (that's figurative!).

There are many different kinds of figurative language. In *Voice Lessons*, we will concentrate on the following figures of speech: metaphor, simile, personification, hyperbole, understatement, metonymy, symbolism, and irony. Although you have undoubtedly experienced these figures of speech before, it is helpful to examine figurative language more deeply, to understand how great writers use figurative language, and to discover how you can use figurative language effectively in your own writing.

Metaphors and similes are used to compare things that are not usually seen as similar. Metaphors imply the comparison, and similes state the comparison directly. Suppose, for example, you've just watched Kerry win the 100-meter sprint at a track event. To make this idea into a metaphor, you could say, *Kerry flew around the track!* Of course, she didn't fly; the metaphor captures the speed and grace of her run by comparing it to the flight of a bird or perhaps a fast jet. The comparison between the race and flight is not directly stated. Instead, the comparison is implied or suggested. It identifies her performance in the race with flight. A metaphor implies a comparison in order to bring fresh, rich meaning to writing.

A simile is a comparison, too. With a simile, however, the comparison is directly stated. To make the race metaphor into a simile, you make the comparison explicit: *Kerry ran like a bird in flight.* It is still nonliteral language—running is not flying—but with a simile you come right out and state the comparison. Similes have signal words that give you a hint a simile is coming. These words include *as, like, **than, similar to**,* and *resembles*. Be careful, though. These words don't always indicate similes. If I say, *As I went to the store, it started to rain,* it is not a simile.

Neither is the sentence, *I look like my mother.* These are literal statements. To be a simile or a metaphor, the comparison must be of essentially unlike things.

Metaphors and similes have <u>literal terms</u> and <u>figurative terms</u>.

- The <u>literal term</u> is what we are comparing to something else. It's what's real; it means what it is. For example, the literal term in the metaphor, *Kerry flew around the track!* is Kerry's running. We are really talking about her race.

- The <u>figurative term</u> is what is being compared to the literal term. The figurative term means something other than itself, something nonliteral. The figurative term in the metaphor is *flight.* She didn't fly in the race, but the race had some flightlike qualities that help the reader understand just how fast she ran.

<u>Personification</u> is a special kind of metaphor that gives human qualities to something that is not human, such as an animal, an object, or an idea. For example, if we say, *The old hickory tree sighed sadly in the wind*, we are using personification. A tree can't really sigh or be sad. We are giving the tree characteristics of a person. Personification, since it is a kind of metaphor, has a literal and figurative term. In this example, the literal term is the hickory tree (it really is a tree), and the figurative term is a sad person. In personification the figurative term is always a person.

<u>Hyperbole</u> is an exaggeration in the service of truth. The key to hyperbole is the part about truth. Hyperboles must be founded on truth to be meaningful. If I say, *I'm so tired I could sleep for a week*, I am using a hyperbole. I'm not in a coma, and I couldn't really sleep for a week, but it feels that way. The truth lies in the extent of the tiredness. Hyperboles add interest, sometimes humor, and emphasis to what you're trying to say.

<u>Understatement</u> is a figure of speech that intentionally makes something important or serious seem less so. With understatement, the reader expects one kind of response but gets another. If, for example, you got into four Ivy League colleges, someone asked how your college applications were going, and you replied, *not bad*, you are using understatement. Understatement can emphasize what is understated by the contrast between what is expected and what the writer says. It can also lend dignity to a response, as you will see in the lessons.

<u>Metonymy</u> is a figure of speech that uses a part of something or something closely related to represent the thing itself. For example, when, in Shakespeare's *Julius Caesar*, Mark Antony says, *Friends, Romans, countrymen, lend me your ears,* he is using metonymy. He wants them to listen, not give him their ears! Metonymy is another way to deepen meaning.

<u>Symbolism</u> is the use of an object, action, or word that stands for something else, usually a complex, abstract idea. Unlike metaphors and similes, symbols do not get their meaning through comparison. Instead, they derive meaning through association, often historical, of a concrete object or word with an idea. For example, there is nothing intrinsically romantic about the human heart; but throughout history it has been associated with love in literature and art. It has thus come to symbolize love through continued association.

Like metaphors and similes, symbols have more than a literal meaning. A symbol, however, often means itself *and* something else. In other words, symbols can actually appear in the text, but they also represent an idea or abstraction. The meaning can be both literal and figurative.

For example, a rainbow is a symbol of hope. If we were reading a story about a group of people who survive a shipwreck by floating through dangerous waters on a raft, and the story ends with a description of a rainbow over an island in the distance, we would know that the people will make it to the island. The rainbow lets us know that there is hope for the future. It *is* a rainbow, but it is *also* the symbol of hope. That is one difference between a symbol and a metaphor or simile. In a metaphor or simile, the figurative term is only something else. We can say, *Her face darkened like an impending thunderstorm*, but it's never a literal thunderstorm. With symbols, however, you have the actual rainbow, thunderstorm (or whatever the object is that has the figurative meaning), and its deeper, or associated, meaning.

Symbols can also be metaphoric. When William Blake writes, *O Rose, thou art sick*, he is using a metaphor. However, the rose has become a symbol of love and beauty through historical repetition and association. So the symbol is the rose and the metaphor is the comparison between his love and a sick rose. The key to symbols is the associated idea that underlies them. Like all figures of speech, symbols add substance and depth to writing.

Irony is the use of language to establish a contrast between what is actually said and what is intended or meant. Irony is figurative because the language is not literal: The surface and underlying meaning are not the same. There are two basic kinds of irony: verbal and situational. With verbal irony, what is stated is the opposite of what is meant. We use verbal irony all of the time in speech. When the cafeteria has just served a tasteless and overcooked meal and you say, *Great lunch*, you are using verbal irony. You are saying one thing and meaning the opposite. Like all figures of speech, verbal irony should not be taken literally.

A special case of verbal irony is sarcasm. Sarcasm is irony that is meant to hurt. For example, if it's storming outside and you want to go for a swim, you might say, *Nice day, isn't it?* That is ironic but not sarcastic. It isn't a nice day, but your statement doesn't hurt anyone. If, however, someone in your class just got a terrible grade on an oral presentation and you say, *Nice job*, you are being both ironic and sarcastic. The presentation wasn't successful, and your comment is intended to hurt. Sarcasm is always ironic, but irony is not always sarcastic.

Situational irony exists in the context of a narrative. It occurs when events end up in a very different way than what is expected. Here is an example: *A high school junior named Linda is certain she is going to the prom, a month away, with her boyfriend. She is so certain that she has already bought her dress and made an appointment to have her hair done. In school one day, Linda makes fun of a classmate, Sarah, who does not have a date for the prom. Of course, Sarah is hurt, but she just walks away. Two days before the prom, Linda learns that her boyfriend is taking Sarah to the prom, not her. Linda has no date to the prom after all.* This is situational irony. Linda makes fun of Sarah for not having a date for the prom, but it turns out that she, not Sarah, has no date for the prom.

Irony is sometimes difficult to understand. It can be funny or serious, affectionate or contemptuous. You have to read carefully and watch the way the words and details are used. If you misunderstand the irony, you can miss the whole point of what you are reading.

Imagery is the verbal representation of sensory experience. Writers create images using all five senses: sight (visual imagery), sound (auditory imagery), touch (tactile imagery), taste (gustatory imagery), and smell (olfactory imagery). Visual imagery and auditory imagery are most common, but writers experiment with a variety of images and even purposefully intermingle the senses (giving smells a color, for example). Imagery depends on both diction and detail: An image's success in producing a sensory experience results from the specificity of the author's diction and choice of detail. Imagery contributes to voice by evoking vivid experience, conveying specific emotion, and suggesting a particular idea.

Imagery itself is not figurative, but it may be used to impart figurative or symbolic meaning. For example, the parched earth can be an image *and* a metaphor for a character's despair; a bird's flight can be an image *and* a metaphor for freedom. Traditional images typically have a long, literary history and have become symbolic. A river, for example, is often associated with life's journey. Traditional images are rarely disassociated from their historic meaning. I encourage you to examine the traditional meanings of images, the departure from tradition, and the effect of both on meaning. You should also learn to recognize and analyze nontraditional and nonfigurative imagery used to influence and sharpen reader perception.

Syntax refers to the way words are arranged within sentences. Although the basic structure of the English sentence is prescribed (there must be a subject and verb; word order cannot be random), there is great latitude in its execution. How writers control and manipulate the sentence is a strong determiner of voice and imparts personality to the writing. Syntax includes word order, sentence length, sentence focus, and punctuation.

Most English sentences follow a subject-verb-object/complement pattern. Deviating from the expected word order can serve to startle the reader and draw attention to the sentence. This, in turn, emphasizes the unusual sentence's message. There are several ways to change normal word order:

- Inverting subject and verb (<u>Am</u> I ever sorry!);
- Placing a complement at the beginning of a sentence (<u>Hungry</u> he is.);
- Placing an object in front of a verb (<u>Chocolate</u> I like—not vanilla.).

Good writers shift between conformity and nonconformity, preventing reader complacency and boredom without using unusual sentence structure to the point of distraction.

Another aspect of syntax is <u>sentence length</u>. Writers vary sentence length to forestall boredom and control emphasis. A short sentence following a much longer sentence shifts the reader's attention, which emphasizes the meaning and importance of the short sentence. Many modern writers put key ideas in short sentences. However, this has not always been so. Practice will help you learn to examine sentence length and look for the relationship between length and emphasis in works from different historical periods.

Sentence length contributes to variation and emphasis among sentences. <u>Sentence focus</u> deals with variation and emphasis within a sentence. In the English sentence, main ideas are usually expressed in main-clause positions. However, main-clause placement often varies, and this placement determines the writer's focal point. Sentence focus is generally achieved by syntactic tension and repetition.

Syntactic tension is the withholding of syntactic closure (completion of grammatical structure) until the end of a sentence. Sentences that delay closure are called *periodic sentences*. Periodic sentences carry high tension and interest: The reader must wait until the end of the sentence to understand the meaning. For example, note that the main idea of the following sentence is completed at the end of the sentence: *As long as we ignore our young people and refuse to dedicate the necessary time and money to their care, <u>we will fail to solve the problem of school violence</u>*. The emphasis here is on the problem.

In contrast, sentences that reach syntactical closure early (loose sentences) relieve tension and allow the reader to explore the rest of the sentence without urgency. Note the difference in tension when we change the sentence to a loose sentence: *We will fail to solve the problem of school violence as long as we ignore our young people and refuse to dedicate the necessary time and money to their care*. The emphasis here is on the cause of failure.

Repetition is another way writers achieve sentence focus. Purposeful repetition of a word, phrase, or clause emphasizes the repeated structure and focuses the reader's attention on its meaning. Writers can also repeat parallel grammatical forms such as infinitives, gerunds, and prepositional phrases. This kind of repetition balances parallel ideas and gives them equal weight.

Punctuation is used to reinforce meaning, construct effect, and express the writer's voice. Of particular interest in shaping voice are the semicolon, colon, and dash.

- The semicolon gives equal weight to two or more independent clauses in a sentence. The resulting syntactical balance reinforces parallel ideas and imparts equal importance to both (or all) of the clauses.

- The colon directs your attention to the words that follow. It is also used between independent clauses if the second summarizes or explains the first. A colon sets the expectation that important, closely related information will follow, and words after the colon are emphasized.

- The dash marks a sudden change in thought or tone, sets off a brief summary, or sets off a parenthetical part of the sentence. The dash often conveys a casual tone.

You will learn to analyze punctuation through careful reading and practice.

Tone is the expression of attitude. It is the writer's (or narrator's) implied attitude toward his or her subject and/or audience. The writer creates tone by selection (diction) and arrangement (syntax) of words and by purposeful use of details, figurative language, and imagery. The reader perceives tone by examining these elements. Tone sets the relationship between reader and writer. As the emotion growing out of the material and connecting the material to the reader, tone is the hallmark of the writer's personality.

Understanding tone is requisite to understanding meaning. Such understanding is the key to perceiving the author's mood and making the connection between the author's thought and expression. Identifying and analyzing tone requires careful reading, sensitivity to diction and syntax, and understanding of detail selection, figures of speech, and imagery. Tone is as varied as human experience; and as with human experience, familiarity and thought pave the way to understanding.

Some of the lessons you will encounter are difficult. You may want to reach for your phone or tablet to see what others have written and said. I urge you to resist this temptation. Now is a time in your life when you are free to be an intellectual, to participate in honest discussions, to think deeply and even profoundly. Accept the challenge of reading and rereading, of contemplation, of trying out new styles of writing. Your life will be immeasurably enriched.

I wish you well as you work with *Voice Lessons*. May you come to understand and wield these powerful tools of the writer, and may your own voices ring strong and true.

—*Nancy Dean*

Detecting Voice

Diction

Consider:

I went out to the hazel wood,
Because a **fire** was in my head,
And cut and peeled a hazel wand,
And hooked a berry to a thread;
And when white moths were on the wing,
And **moth-like** stars were flickering out,
I dropped the berry in a stream
And caught a little silver trout.

W. B. Yeats, "The Song of Wandering Aengus," *The Wind Among the Reeds*

Discuss:

1. Read line two carefully. Name at least three associations with the word *fire* that make it the perfect word to describe the narrator's state of mind.

2. What picture comes to your mind when you read *moth-like stars*? How would it change the impact of the line if Yeats had written the line this way:

   And twinkling stars were going out

Apply:

List three compound adjectives (like *moth-like*) that can be used to describe a dark cloud. Each adjective should connote a different feeling about the cloud. Discuss your list with a partner. Share one of the best compound adjectives with the class.

Diction

Consider:

Close by the fire sat an old man whose countenance was **furrowed** with distress.

James Boswell, Boswell's London Journal 1762–1763

Discuss:

1. What does the word *furrowed* connote about the man's distress?

2. How would the impact of the sentence be changed if *furrowed* were changed to *lined*?

Apply:

Write a sentence using a verb to describe a facial expression. Imply through your verb choice that the expression is intense. Use Boswell's sentence as a model. Share your sentence with a partner.

Diction

Consider:

> . . . then Satan first knew pain,
> And writh'd him to and fro convolv'd; so sore
> The **grinding** sword with **discontinuous** wound
> Pass'd through him.

John Milton, *Paradise Lost*, Book VI

Discuss:

1. By using the word *grinding*, what does Milton imply about the pain inflicted by the sword?

2. What does *discontinuous* mean? How does the use of *discontinuous* reinforce the idea of a *grinding* sword?

Apply:

Think about the motion of a *grinding* sword, a *slashing* sword, and a *piercing* sword. Discuss the context in which a writer might use the three different kinds of swords.

Diction

Consider:

I distinguished Mr. Heathcliff's step, restlessly measuring the floor, and he frequently broke the silence by a deep inspiration, resembling a groan. He muttered **detached** words also; the only one I could catch was the name of Catherine, coupled with some wild term of endearment or suffering; and spoken as one would speak to a person present; low and earnest, and **wrung** from the depth of his soul.

Emily Brontë, *Wuthering Heights*

Discuss:

1. This passage comes at the end of the novel when Heathcliff is feeling the pull of death and is longing to join Catherine in death. The narrator calls Heathcliff's words *detached*. What does this word reveal about Heathcliff's mental state?

2. Look up the word *wring*. The action of this verb requires considerable effort. Who is doing the wringing? How does this word help the reader participate in the atmosphere created by the passage?

Apply:

Work with a partner or in a small group. Substitute the following words for *wrung* in the passage above and explain how each new word changes the meaning and feeling of the passage.

- taken
- slipped
- offered
- sprung
- leaked

Consider:

This great Nation will endure as it has endured, will revive and will prosper. So, first of all, let me assert my firm belief that the only thing we have to fear is fear itself—**nameless**, **unreasoning**, **unjustified** terror which paralyzes needed efforts to **convert** retreat into advance.

President Franklin Delano Roosevelt, First Inaugural Address

Discuss:

1. What is the purpose of this passage? President Roosevelt defines fear as *nameless, unreasoning, unjustified terror*. How does each of these adjectives contribute to the purpose of the passage?

2. How would it change the impact of the passage if Roosevelt had said *terror which paralyzes needed efforts to change retreat into advance*?

Apply:

Complete the following sentence frame, defining *trust*. Select words that are clear, concrete, and exact, and use Roosevelt's sentence as a model.

Let me assert my firm belief that the only thing we have to trust is trust itself—

————————————————, ————————————————, ————————————————,

trust [or a strong synonym for *trust*] *which* _____

_____

_____

_____

_____

_____ .

Discussion Suggestions

W. B. Yeats, "The Song of Wandering Aengus," *The Wind Among the Reeds*

1. There are many associations with fire that clarify the narrator's state of mind. Fire is unpredictable and hard to control. It is also hot and capable of great harm. Fire is also complex, with different levels of heat and color. Several of the colors of fire—red, orange, and yellow—are associated with vitality, disorder, and energy, all qualities that are part of the *fire* in the narrator's head, making his state of mind literally combustible. Like fire, the narrator's mind is out of control and in need of quenching. Although fire can also be a comfort, here it is contrasted with fishing in the woods, which is presented as soothing.

2. *Moth-like stars* seem fragile and ephemeral, blinking then disappearing, like insects of the night. This compound adjective also links the line to the *white moths* in the previous line, intensifying the experience of both the moths and the stars. The new line lacks freshness and precision of effect. The reader is left with a banal description that carries none of the power and movement of the original line. The new line also loses the connection to the white moths, a powerful connection that brings the reader into the experience of the poem.

James Boswell, *Boswell's London Journal 1762–1763*

1. A furrow is a deep wrinkle. It connotes acute distress. The word *furrowed* is specific and concrete, which focuses the reader's attention and gives emphasis to the distress.

2. The sentence would lack the focus and emphasis of the original. A *lined* countenance shows less distress than a *furrowed* one.

John Milton, *Paradise Lost*, **Book VI**

1. *Grinding* means to crush or pulverize by friction. A *grinding* sword thus does not produce a clean cut. Instead, it uses a rubbing or crushing motion to inflict its injury. The implication is one of heightened pain brought about by rough motion, the turning and crushing of the sword.

2. *Discontinuous* means marked by breaks or interruptions. The word reinforces the idea of a grinding sword by echoing the motion of the sword. Grinding is an intermittent action, so the wound is discontinuous. The pain is also echoed in the diction. Relief from intermittent pain carries with it the expectation of more pain: Even periods of rest are painful.

Emily Brontë, *Wuthering Heights*

1. Just as his words are disconnected or fragmented, Heathcliff is becoming separated from everything in his life. His words are detached from meaning, all words except for *Catherine*; and, like his words, his thoughts are detached from life. He is ready to disconnect and die.

2. The wringing of Heathcliff's words *from the depth of his soul* could be an action of Heathcliff himself in an attempt to contact the spirit of Catherine and join her, or it could be an action of Catherine as she tries to help Heathcliff cross over into her world. The ambiguity of the word helps create the atmosphere of mystery, darkness, and confusion. It infuses the scene with potential violence (the words could have been *coaxed* from the depth of his soul) and reinforces the detachment of Heathcliff from his life.

President Franklin Delano Roosevelt, First Inaugural Address

1. Help students understand that the purpose of the passage is to rally the American people, to fix their resolve in a time of economic desperation (The Great Depression), and to comfort them with a view of America's enduring and prosperous future. President Roosevelt does this by defining fear and dismissing it. Fear is *nameless*, an abstraction not even identifiable. Fear is *unreasoning*, not based on logical, intellectual thought. Fear is *unjustified*, unfounded, and inexcusable. These words support the purpose of the passage by framing fear as an obstacle that should be brushed aside. Fear is an irrational abstraction, one that should be disregarded as America advances toward a prosperous future.

2. *Change* is a much weaker verb in this context. To change something is to modify it. It may or may not be permanent. To *convert*, however, is to alter something's nature or beliefs. Roosevelt is not calling for mere change. Instead, he is calling for a conversion, a transformation. He has chosen the perfect word to stir his audience and move his people to action.

Detail

Consider:

Whenever he was so fortunate as to have near him a hare that had been kept too long, or a meat pie made with rancid butter, he gorged himself with such violence that his veins swelled, and the moisture broke out on his forehead.

Thomas Babington Macaulay, *Life of Samuel Johnson*

Discuss:

1. What effect does the detail (the spoiled hare, the rancid butter, the swollen veins, the sweaty forehead) have on the reader?

2. How would the meaning of the sentence be changed by ending it after *himself*?

Apply:

Write a sentence describing someone with disgusting eating habits. It must be one grammatically correct sentence, and it must contain at least three vivid details.

Detail

Consider:

He went on till he came to the first milestone, which stood in the bank, half way up a steep hill. He rested his basket on the top of the stone, placed his elbows on it, and gave way to a convulsive twitch, which was worse than a sob, because it was so hard and so dry.

Thomas Hardy, *The Mayor of Casterbridge: A Story of a Man of Character*

Discuss:

1. How do the details in this passage prepare you for the *convulsive twitch* at the end of the passage?

2. This passage does not describe the character's face at all. What effect does this lack of detail have on the reader?

Apply:

Plan a pantomime of the scene described in this passage, and perform it for the class. After several people have performed their pantomimes, discuss the facial expressions they used in their pantomimes. Discuss the similarities and differences and how they relate to the use of detail in the passage.

Detail

Consider:

How fine it is to enter some old town, walled and turreted, just at approach of nightfall, or to come to some straggling village, with the lights streaming through the surrounding gloom; and then, after inquiring for the best entertainment that the place affords, to "take one's ease at one's inn"!

William Hazlitt, "On Going a Journey," *Table Talk: Essays on Men and Manners*

Discuss:

1. What details support the generalization, *How fine it is*?

2. What feelings are evoked by the details of the town (*old, walled, turreted*)? How does this selection of detail communicate Hazlitt's attitude toward the town?

Apply:

Imagine going to a motel after a long day on the road. The motel is the only place to sleep in town, and the next town is 200 miles away. The motel is old and dirty; your room is shabby and dark. Plan a brief monologue that expresses your attitude toward this room. Include specific references to the details that both produce and reveal your attitude. Perform your monologue for the class.

Detail

Consider:

The wild gander leads his flock through the cool night,

Ya-honk he says, and sounds it down to me like an invitation,

The pert may suppose it meaningless, but I listening close,

Find its purpose and place up there toward the wintery sky.

The sharp-hoof'd moose of the north, the cat on the house-sill, the chickadee, the prairie-dog,

The litter of the grunting sow as they tug at her teats,

The brood of the turkey-hen and she with her half-spread wings,

I see in them and myself the same old law.

Walt Whitman, "Song of Myself," *Leaves of Grass*

Discuss:

1. What is the conclusion of the last line? Which details in the passage support this conclusion?

2. The animals in these stanzas are specific and detailed. In contrast, the ambience (*the cool night*, *the wintery sky*) is more general. What attitude is revealed by this difference?

Apply:

Rewrite the passage, describing the night and the sky in great detail and the animals in general terms. Read your version to the class and lead a discussion about how this change shifts the meaning of the passage.

Detail

Consider:

In fact right behind her Gabriel could be seen piloting Freddy Malins across the landing. The latter, a young man of about forty, was of Gabriel's size and build, with very round shoulders. His face was fleshy and pallid, touched with colour only at the thick hanging lobes of his ears and at the wide wings of his nose. He had coarse features, a blunt nose, a convex and receding brow, tumid and protruded lips. His heavy-lidded eyes and the disorder of his scanty hair made him look sleepy.

James Joyce, "The Dead," *Dubliners*

Discuss:

1. Joyce uses many specific details to describe Freddy's physical appearance. Fill in the chart below and indicate (X) whether each detail is objective (making an observation) or evaluative (making a judgment).

Detail	Objective	Evaluative

2. What is Joyce's attitude toward Freddy? Which specific details reveal this attitude?

Apply:

Write a paragraph describing a character's personality by describing his or her physical traits. Do not make any direct statements about his or her personality or character. Instead, use detail about appearance to capture character. Read your paragraph to a partner and discuss which physical traits are stereotypes and which traits are valid indications of character.

Discussion Suggestions

Detail

Thomas Babington Macaulay,
Life of Samuel Johnson

1. The spoiled hare and the rancid butter add specificity to the general idea that Johnson will eat anything. The other details create a precise, and rather violent, picture of Johnson's disgusting eating habits. In your discussion with students, it would be helpful to provide this information about Johnson: In contrast to his personal slovenliness, Johnson was a brilliant writer, conversationalist, and the first English language lexicographer. The details in this passage set up a sharp contrast between his personal habits and his prodigious mind and accomplishments. Understanding this contrast might liven up the discussion.

2. It takes away the sentence's power to bring the reader into the scene. It reduces the reader's involvement and lessens the power to shape the reader's attitude toward Johnson.

Thomas Hardy, *The Mayor of Casterbridge: A Story of a Man of Character*

1. The details of this passage suggest a long, tiring journey. He stops at the *first milestone*, which suggests there will be more. The milestone is *half way up a steep hill*, which suggests he has a long way to go, and the going will be difficult. He has to rest, which again suggests a difficult journey; and he rests in a stooped position, which suggests dejection. All of these details work together to create a picture of weariness and misery, which culminates in the *convulsive twitch* at the end of the sentence.

2. The lack of detail about the character's face is an understatement. The lack of detail is in sharp contrast to the intensity of the character's melancholy. The focus is on the character's *convulsive twitch*, his internal pain, his utter dejection. Elaborate description would turn this pure pain into sentimentality. The lack of detail about the character's face thus makes the description of the character's pain sharper and more meaningful.

William Hazlitt, "On Going a Journey," *Table Talk: Essays on Men and Manners*

1. Details that support the generalization, *How fine it is*, include entering a town that is *walled and turreted*, *lights streaming through the surrounding gloom*, and *the best entertainment that the place affords*. These details work together to create a feeling of warmth and comfort after a hard day's travel.

2. The details create a romantic picture of a quaint town from another era. That the town is walled and turreted could create a feeling of foreboding and fear; but these details are preceded by an assertion of a *fine* experience, so they create instead a feeling of welcoming protection. Hazlitt's attitude is thus established: This town will welcome him with warmth, protection, rest, and entertainment.

Walt Whitman, "Song of Myself," *Leaves of Grass*

1. The conclusion of the last line is that the *I* or persona of the poem is at one with all creatures and subject to the same laws: life, procreation, and ultimately death. Details that support this conclusion are the perceived invitation of the wild gander; the variety of animal life in line 5 (the <u>lack</u> of detail in this line indicates an equality of the animal forms, the belief that no animal is more important than another); the sow with her young; and the turkey-hen with her brood. The persona of the poem gives equal weight to his own experience and the experience of other animals.

2. The difference in the use of detail reveals a difference in attitude. Animals and humans are enmeshed in rhythms of birth, life, and death. The sky and the night are impersonal and impassive: They do not embody the life and death rhythms of animals. Since the sky and the night are not the focus of these lines, they are best described in general terms. Extensive detail is reserved for what is given higher value in the poem.

James Joyce, "The Dead," *Dubliners*

1. The chart below may be of help in discussing this question. In general, objective details carry no strong connotation and reveal little about character. Evaluative details carry strong connotations and reveal insights about character. The evaluative details in this passage indicate a weakness in Freddy's character by describing his physical appearance as *fleshy* and *coarse*. His face literally sags and indicates (since he is not old) a lack of resolve. Students may disagree as to which details are evaluative, which is excellent and may generate lively discussion.

2. Joyce's attitude toward Freddy is critical. Freddy's fleshy, pale face indicates weakness and unhealthiness. The touch of color on his nose indicates an over-indulgence in drink, and the coarse features indicate lack of mental and social refinement. The sleepy look of his heavy-lidded eyes and his disordered, scanty hair reveal a character ill-equipped to carry on normal intellectual and social interactions.

Detail	Objective	Evaluative
a young man of about forty	X	
of Gabriel's size and build	X	
with very round shoulders	X	
His face was fleshy and pallid		X
[His face was] touched with colour only at the thick hanging lobes of his ears and at the wide wings of his nose		X
He had coarse features, a blunt nose, a convex and receding brow, tumid and protruded lips		X
heavy-lidded eyes		X
disorder of his scanty hair		X

Figurative Language

Consider:

The narrow creek was like a ditch: tortuous, fabulously deep; filled with gloom under the thin strip of pure and shining blue of the heaven. Immense trees soared up, invisible behind the festooned draperies of creepers. Here and there, near the glistening blackness of the water, a twisted root of some tall tree showed amongst the tracery of small ferns, black and dull, writhing and motionless, like an arrested snake.

Joseph Conrad, "The Lagoon," *Cornhill Magazine*

Discuss:

1. In the first sentence of this passage, Conrad says *The narrow creek was like a ditch*. Is this a simile? If so, what are the literal and figurative terms? What do we learn about the creek through this comparison?

2. In the third sentence, he says *a twisted root of some tall tree showed amongst the tracery of small ferns, black and dull, writhing and motionless, like an arrested snake*. Is this a simile? If so, what are the literal and figurative terms? What do we learn about the setting through this comparison?

Apply:

Write a paragraph describing an outdoor scene at your school or in your neighborhood. In your description, use a comparison that is not a simile and one that is. Your simile should give insight into the literal term by comparing it to the figurative term. Both comparisons should help create the mood of your paragraph, as they do in Conrad's paragraph. Share your paragraph with a classmate.

Figurative Language

Consider:

Rather than love, than money, than fame, give me truth. I sat at a table
where were rich food and wine in abundance, and obsequious attendance, but
sincerity and truth were not; and I went away hungry from the inhospitable
board. The hospitality was as cold as the ices. I thought that there was no
need of ice to freeze them. They talked to me of the age of the wine and the
fame of the vintage; but I thought of an older, a newer, and purer wine, of a
more glorious vintage, which they had not got, and could not buy. The style,
the house and grounds and "entertainment" pass for nothing with me. I
called on the king, but he made me wait in his hall, and conducted like a man
incapacitated for hospitality. There was a man in my neighborhood who lived
in a hollow tree. His manners were truly regal. I should have done better had
I called on him.

Henry David Thoreau, *Walden*

Discuss:

1. In this excerpt from the conclusion of *Walden*, Thoreau talks about the importance of
   truth. He uses an extended metaphor to make his point. First, he talks about the lavish
   manners and hospitality of the rich. The literal term of the first part of the metaphor
   is manners and hospitality devoid of truth. What is the figurative term? What does the
   metaphor reveal about Thoreau's attitude toward truth?

2. Thoreau goes further and extends the metaphor with another literal term: manners and
   hospitality accompanied by truth. What is the figurative term here? In your own words,
   summarize Thoreau's attitude toward truth and manners/hospitality.

Apply:

Think about a time when a birthday party was spoiled by something that had nothing to
do with the food or the presents. Talk about this with a classmate. Now write a paragraph
that uses a metaphor to capture what spoiled the party. Extend that metaphor to capture
what could have made the party perfect. Be certain to have clear literal and figurative
terms. Use Thoreau's paragraph as a model.

Figurative Language

Consider:

"I have known myself to be divided from Edward for ever, without hearing one circumstance that could make me less desire the connection. Nothing has proved him unworthy; nor has anything declared him indifferent to me. I have had to contend against the unkindness of his sister, and the insolence of his mother; and have suffered the punishment of an attachment, without enjoying its advantages. And all this has been going on at a time, when, as you know too well, it has not been my only unhappiness. If you can think me capable of ever feeling, surely you may suppose that I have suffered *now*. . . ."

Marianne was quite subdued.

"Oh! Elinor," she cried, "you have made me hate myself for ever. How barbarous have I been to you!—you, who have been my only comfort, who have borne with me in all my misery, who have seemed to be only suffering for me! Is this my gratitude? Is this the only return I can make you?"

Jane Austen, Sense and Sensibility

Discuss:

1. In this passage from *Sense and Sensibility*, Marianne has accused her sister Elinor of not having suffered for love. Elinor's reply is in the first paragraph above. Is the language of this paragraph figurative or literal? What effect does this have on Marianne and on the reader?

2. Analyze the use of hyperbole in Marianne's reply, identifying each example and what it reveals about Marianne's character. How does the use of hyperbole help the reader understand the different natures of the two sisters?

Apply:

Write two paragraphs about the end of an exciting sporting event. In the first paragraph, clearly describe what happened. Use strong and vivid imagery, but do not use any figurative language. In the second paragraph, describe the same event using hyperbole. Share your paragraphs with a classmate, and discuss the different impact each paragraph has on the reader.

Figurative language

Consider:

Kant has written a treatise on *The Vital Powers*; but I should like to write a dirge on them, since their lavish use in the form of knocking, hammering, and tumbling things about has made the whole of my life a daily torment. Certainly there are people, nay, very many, who will smile at this, because they are not sensitive to noise; it is precisely these people, however, who are not sensitive to argument, thought, poetry or art, in short, to any kind of intellectual impression. . . . I should explain the subject we are treating in this way: If a big diamond is cut up into pieces, it immediately loses its value as a whole; or if an army is scattered or divided into small bodies, it loses all its power; and in the same way a great intellect has no more power than an ordinary one as soon as it is interrupted, disturbed, distracted, or diverted; for its superiority entails that it concentrates all its strength on one point and object, just as a concave mirror concentrates all the rays of light thrown upon it. Noisy interruption prevents this concentration.

Arthur Schopenhauer, "On Noise," *The Essays of Schopenhauer*

Discuss:

1. There are three similes in this passage. Identify the similes and their literal and figurative terms. What makes them similes rather than metaphors?

2. What is the purpose of using similes rather than literal explanation in this passage?

Apply:

Think about something that really bothers you. It could be something inconsequential like the sound of someone snapping gum, or it could be something significant like someone polluting the environment. Talk about this in a small group. With your group, select two or three of the irritants you discussed and write similes for them. Your similes should provide insight into the nature and importance of the annoyance. Share your similes with the class.

Figurative Language

Consider:

Three out of the ten years since I left you, I spent as a common laborer on the wharves of New Bedford, Massachusetts. It was there I earned my first free dollar. It was mine. I could spend it as I pleased. I could buy hams or herring with it, without asking any odds of anybody. That was a precious dollar to me. You remember when I used to make seven, or eight, or even nine dollars a week in Baltimore, you would take every cent of it from me every Saturday night, saying that I belonged to you, and my earnings also. I never liked this conduct on your part—to say the best, I thought it a little mean. I would not have served you so.

Frederick Douglass, "Letter to My Old Master, Thomas Auld," *My Bondage and My Freedom*

Discuss:

1. In the second sentence of this passage, Douglass uses metonymy. Identify the metonym, clarify why it is an example of metonymy, and explain how the use of metonymy adds to the reader's understanding of the passage.

2. Reread the passage and then closely examine the following sentence: *I never liked this conduct on your part—to say the best, I thought it a little mean.* Does his calling Auld's taking of his money *a little mean* [cheap] surprise you? This is an example of understatement. How does the use of understatement add to the power and dignity of the passage?

Apply:

Write a brief letter to your local newspaper objecting to a school or community policy. In your letter, use understatement rather than hyperbole or outrage to make your point. Use the excerpt from Douglass' letter as a model.

Figurative language

Consider:

Turning towards the hearth, where the two logs had fallen apart, and sent forth only a red uncertain glimmer, he seated himself on his fireside chair, and was stooping to push his logs together, when, to his blurred vision, it seemed as if there were gold on the floor in front of the hearth. Gold!—his own gold—brought back to him as mysteriously as it had been taken away! He felt his heart begin to beat violently, and for a few moments he was unable to stretch out his hand and grasp the restored treasure. The heap of gold seemed to glow and get larger beneath his agitated gaze. He leaned forward at last, and stretched forth his hand; but instead of the hard coin with the familiar resisting outline, his fingers encountered soft warm curls. In utter amazement, Silas fell on his knees and bent his head low to examine the marvel: it was a sleeping child—a round, fair thing, with soft yellow rings all over its head.

George Eliot, *Silas Marner*

Discuss:

1. *Silas Marner* is a novel about redemption through love. Silas Marner, the protagonist of the novel, is falsely accused of a theft; and he is cast out by his community. Despondent and alone, he becomes a miser, hoarding gold as his only pleasure. As the novel progresses, his gold is stolen and Marner falls deeper into despair. This passage captures a pivotal moment in the novel, when a child enters his life and transforms it. Identify the central metaphor in the passage and its literal and figurative terms.

2. How does the use of a metaphor add to the intensity and meaning of the passage?

Apply:

Here is a list of things that you may or may not value. With a partner, write a metaphor for the entries on the list. Your metaphors should give fresh insight into the worth (or lack of worth) you place on each entry.

- a pet you had as a child
- your phone
- time with your friends
- travel to new places
- a time you accomplished something you didn't think you could accomplish

Figurative Language

Consider:

A flower was offered to me,
    Such a flower as May never bore;
But I said, 'I've a pretty rose tree,'
    And I passed the sweet flower o'er.

Then I went to my pretty rose tree,
    To tend her by day and by night;
But my rose turned away with jealousy,
    And her thorns were my only delight.

William Blake, "My Pretty Rose Tree," *Songs of Experience*

Discuss:

1. In the second stanza, Blake personifies the rose tree. What are the literal and figurative terms of the personification? What does the use of personification add to the reader's understanding of the poem?

2. The rose is also a symbol. What does it symbolize, and how does the use of symbolism contribute to the reader's understanding of the poem?

Apply:

Brainstorm with your class a list of symbols that are commonly used in literature. Remember that a symbol is both itself and something other than itself. For example, the U.S. flag is a flag, but it also stands for our country. Now choose one symbol from the list and write a four-line poem that uses the symbol in its literal and figurative sense and imparts fresh meaning to the poem.

Figurative Language

Consider:

It is a melancholy object to those, who walk through this great town, or travel in the country, when they see the streets, the roads and cabin-doors crowded with beggars of the female sex, followed by three, four, or six children, all in rags, and importuning every passenger for an alms. These mothers instead of being able to work for their honest livelihood, are forced to employ all their time in stroling to beg sustenance for their helpless infants who, as they grow up, either turn thieves for want of work, or leave their dear native country, to fight for the Pretender in Spain, or sell themselves to the Barbadoes.

I think it is agreed by all parties, that this prodigious number of children in the arms, or on the backs, or at the heels of their mothers, and frequently of their fathers, is in the present deplorable state of the kingdom, a very great additional grievance; and therefore whoever could find out a fair, cheap and easy method of making these children sound and useful members of the common-wealth, would deserve so well of the publick, as to have his statue set up for a preserver of the nation. . . .

. . . it is exactly at one year old that I propose to provide for them in such a manner, as, instead of being a charge upon their parents, or the parish, or wanting food and raiment for the rest of their lives, they shall, on the contrary, contribute to the feeding, and partly to the cloathing of many thousands. . . .

I shall now therefore humbly propose my own thoughts, which I hope will not be liable to the least objection.

I have been assured by a very knowing American of my acquaintance in London, that a young healthy child well nursed, is, at a year old, a most delicious nourishing and wholesome food, whether stewed, roasted, baked, or boiled; and I make no doubt that it will equally serve in a fricasie, or a ragoust.

I do therefore humbly offer it to publick consideration, that of the hundred and twenty thousand children, already computed, twenty thousand may be reserved for breed. . . . That the remaining hundred thousand may, at a year old, be offered in sale to the persons of quality and fortune, through the kingdom . . . . A child will make two dishes at an entertainment for friends, and when the family dines alone, the fore or hind quarter will make a reasonable dish, and seasoned with a little pepper or salt, will be very good boiled on the fourth day, especially in winter. . . .

Therefore let no man talk to me of other expedients: Of taxing our absentees at five shillings a pound: Of using neither cloaths, nor houshold furniture, except what is of our own growth and manufacture: Of utterly rejecting the materials and instruments that promote foreign luxury: Of curing the expensiveness of pride, vanity, idleness, and gaming in our women: Of introducing a vein of parsimony, prudence and temperance: Of learning to love our country. . . .

. . . Lastly, of putting a spirit of honesty, industry, and skill into our shop-keepers, who, if a resolution could now be taken to buy only our native goods, would immediately unite to cheat and exact upon us in the price, the measure, and the goodness, nor could ever yet be brought to make one fair proposal of just dealing, though often and earnestly invited to it.

Jonathan Swift, "A Modest Proposal" For preventing the children of poor people in Ireland,
from being a burden on their parents or country, and for making them beneficial to the publick.

Discuss:

1. Jonathan Swift was a champion of social causes. Here he is addressing the terrible poverty of Ireland at the time. Does his "solution" surprise you? How do you know that Swift's "Modest Proposal" is ironic and not the suggestion of a sociopath?

2. Why do you think Swift uses irony instead of writing a straightforward proposal for solving the poverty in Ireland?

Apply:

Write your own "Modest Proposal" for solving a problem in your school. Use irony and precise detail as Swift does. You may want to use ironic humor instead of Swift-like satire.

Figurative language

Consider:

In the long history of the world, only a few generations have been granted the role of defending freedom in its hour of maximum danger. I do not shrink from this responsibility—I welcome it. I do not believe that any of us would exchange places with any other people or any other generation. The energy, the faith, the devotion which we bring to this endeavor will light our country and all who serve it—and the glow from that fire can truly light the world.

President John F. Kennedy, Inaugural Address

Discuss:

1. In the first sentence of this passage, President Kennedy uses metonymy. Identify and explain the metonym. How does the use of metonymy support the strength of Kennedy's assertion that Americans accept the challenge of defending freedom?

2. Discuss the elements of voice in the last sentence of this passage. Consider imagery, symbolism, and metaphor. Remember that these figures of speech sometimes overlap. Just because something is a symbol does not mean that it is not also a metaphor or an image.

Apply:

Rewrite the passage from Kennedy's Inaugural Address and include no figurative language. Share your passage with a small group of classmates, and discuss how the removal of figurative language changes the power of the passage.

Figurative language

Consider:

Let me not to the marriage of true minds
Admit impediments. Love is not love
Which alters when it alteration finds,
Or bends with the remover to remove.
O, no! it is an ever-fixèd mark,
That looks on tempests, and is never shaken;
It is the star to every wandering bark,
Whose worth's unknown, although his height be taken.
Love's not Time's fool, though rosy lips and cheeks
Within his bending sickle's compass come;
Love alters not with his brief hours and weeks,
But bears it out even to the edge of doom.
    If this be error and upon me proved,
    I never writ, nor no man ever loved.

William Shakespeare, Sonnet 116

Discuss:

1. Identify at least one metaphor and one example of personification in this rich and complex sonnet. Name the literal and figurative terms and explain what these figures of speech add to the reader's understanding of the sonnet.

2. Now identify a symbol and an example of metonymy in the sonnet. Explain the significance of these figures of speech and what they contribute to the meaning and power of the sonnet.

Apply:

Write a sonnet (14 lines) about dreams, love, or another topic of your choice. In your sonnet use at least one metaphor, one example of personification, one metonym, and one symbol. If you can write in iambic pentameter and use Shakespeare's rhyme scheme, that would be great; but it's not necessary. You can do a direct modeling of Shakespeare's sonnet if it helps. Share your sonnet with the class.

Discussion Suggestions
Figurative Language

Joseph Conrad, "The Lagoon,"
Cornhill Magazine

1. There may be some lively discussion here, but I would have to contend that *the narrow creek was like a ditch* is not a simile. Remind students that metaphors, similes, and personification are all comparisons of <u>unlike</u> things. The purpose is to give insight into the literal term by comparing it to the figurative term. Here a creek and a ditch are already similar. This is vivid detail and imagery. There is no figurative term. The creek could be called a ditch without a loss of meaning. This comparison adds to the mood and visual acuity of the scene, but it is not figurative.

2. Here we do have a simile. The root is like *an arrested snake*. A root is, of course, not a snake; but by comparing it to a snake, Conrad gives the reader a strong visual image. The literal term is the root and the figurative term is a snake. The snake simile helps the reader participate in the setting of the story. We are familiar with the *writhing and motionless* characteristics of a snake. It helps us visualize the roots. The snake also has a symbolic value, representing evil, temptation, and death. Through the snake as a simile and a symbol, we are able to understand that the setting is ominous: dark, dangerous, and potentially evil. Students may also want to discuss the imagery here, with its darkness and obfuscation.

Henry David Thoreau, *Walden*

1. This complicated metaphor is developed throughout the passage. The figurative term of the first part of the metaphor is multifaceted: an unsatisfying meal that leaves one hungry, ices (a frozen dessert) frozen without ice, and bad wine. The metaphor (and it is a metaphor because it is implied rather than directly stated) here adds insight into the foundation of manners and hospitality for Thoreau: truth. Without truth, the meal, the manners, and the hospitality are nothing. They leave one hungry and cold.

2. The figurative term in the second part of the metaphor is also multifaceted: manners that are regal even in poverty and wine of a *glorious vintage*. Students' explanations of Thoreau's attitude toward truth and manners/hospitality should be something like this: If truth is present, the simplest home and hospitality are regal and rich. Truth is the determiner, not the *style, house and grounds and "entertainment."* If students want to discuss what they think comprises good hospitality, that is fine, but be sure that they don't confuse their own attitudes with Thoreau's! The evidence is in the metaphor.

Jane Austen, *Sense and Sensibility*

1. The language of the first paragraph is literal. There are lots of details and precise diction, but there is no figurative language. The effect on Marianne and the reader is the same. The literal language establishes the causes and results of Elinor's misery. The explanation is clear, concrete, and specific. There is no need for a figure of speech to clarify the fact that Elinor has suffered for love. It convinces through reasons and examples.

2. Remind students that hyperbole is exaggeration in the service of truth. There are several examples here. Marianne says *you have made me hate myself for ever*. Of course, Marianne will not hate herself forever. She won't live forever. Further, she will probably not even hate herself for the rest of her life (or maybe even the rest of the day!). But this exaggeration is in the service of truth. Marianne is angry with herself and wildly exaggerates her self-reproach. In the same way, she calls herself barbarous and calls Elinor *my only comfort*. Marianne is not cruel or uncivilized. She just knows she has been self-centered and acted unfairly. And Elinor could not be her only comfort. Marianne is just recognizing how important her sister has been to her. The style of these two paragraphs clearly reflects the sisters' natures. Elinor is orderly, intellectual, and prudent. Her voice in the first paragraph captures these qualities. Her defense is clear, well supported, and methodical. Marianne, on the other hand, speaks with a voice infused with passion and hyperbole. You can almost feel the tears welling up! She is the passionate and impulsive sister. The sisters' natures are revealed through their language.

Arthur Schopenhauer, "On Noise," *The Essays of Schopenhauer*

1. The three similes in this passage are listed below. In each simile, the literal term is underlined and the figurative term is bracketed.

   a. The intrusion of noise to a great intellect is like [a big diamond that has been cut up into pieces and loses its value].

   b. The intrusion of noise to a great intellect is like [an army that has been scattered into small bodies and loses all of its power].

   c. Superior intellect concentrating on one point or object is like [a concave mirror that concentrates all of the rays of light thrown on it].

   They are similes because the comparison is directly stated rather than implied. The signal words for the similes here are *in the same way*. It would be thought-provoking to discuss the meaning of these similes with students. Schopenhauer is railing against the infringement of noise on his thoughts. It would be interesting to see how your students feel about noise in this raucous culture of ours. How many of them study to music? How many of them keep the TV on in their homes all of the time or talk on the phone as they walk down the street?

2. The similes make Schopenhauer's argument more concrete and specific. In addition, the similes convey attitudes as well as support for his argument. Finally, the similes concentrate and clarify language and lend interest to the writing.

Frederick Douglass, "Letter to My Old Master, Thomas Auld," *My Bondage and My Freedom*

1. The metonym in this sentence is *my first free dollar*. In this figure of speech, Douglass uses a part of something to substitute for the literal thing meant. The dollar is not literally free—no one gave it to him unearned. The *first free dollar* is literally the first dollar he earned and kept as a free man. Like other figures of speech, metonymy adds interest and precision to the language. It also emphasizes the word *free*, which focuses the reader's attention on the contrast between freedom and slavery, dignity and the horrors of oppression.

2. Douglass calls Auld's taking his money *a little mean*. When I read this passage, it took my breath away! Discuss the effect the understatement has on your students. The understatement underscores the power and dignity of Douglass' language. He never rants and raves about the evils he experienced. Instead, he lets the details of his experience speak for themselves. His use of understatement contrasts with the disgust his experiences evoke in the reader and sets him apart from his former master.

George Eliot, *Silas Marner*

1. The central metaphor in the passage is a comparison that identifies the child's golden hair with Marner's lost gold. The literal term is the child's hair and the figurative term is the lost gold.

2. The metaphor is not just a comparison of color. First of all, gold is associated with warmth, abundance, and prosperity—all of which have been lacking in Marner's life. Also, gold, the only thing that has brought any meaning to his life, had been stolen from him. The child who enters his life has golden hair. This identification of the lost gold and the child's hair lets the reader know that there will be a new kind of gold for Marner. It is the more valuable gold that the child brings: the value that comes from love. Rather than explaining this, Eliot uses a metaphor, imparting all of the promise of renewal and a different kind of prosperity. In just a few sentences, Eliot lets the reader understand that Marner gets his gold back but in a different, more precious and enduring form. There is no need to explain further. From this point on, the narrative focus shifts and the new gold offers the promise of happiness.

William Blake, "My Pretty Rose Tree," *Songs of Experience*

1. The literal term is the rose tree. Remind students that the figurative term in personification is always a person. Here, the figurative term is implied: a woman who gets jealous and shows the persona (the narrator) only her hurtful side (thorns). Personification of the rose tree deepens the meaning of the poem and helps the reader make sense of it. Of course a rose tree can't turn away and experience jealousy. But the reader understands that Blake is not really talking about a rose tree. The rose tree represents a woman who sees the persona's temptation in the first stanza and turns away from him, despite his refusal of the temptation. Without personification, the poem makes no sense. The rose tree serves several figurative purposes here. It is an image, adding a rich visual experience to the poem. It is personified as a woman. And it is also a symbol, as we see in question two. The use of figurative language strengthens a poem that seems simple at first and makes the poem complex indeed.

2. The rose is a traditional symbol of beauty, perfection, and love (complete with its thorns). Any reference to a rose in literature brings with it this symbolic meaning. As a symbol, the rose is a literal rose and something more as well. Here the *pretty rose tree* represents beauty, perfection, and love in its purest and most innocent sense. But Blake ends the poem with the thorns, symbolic of the pain of love. Love is spoiled by jealousy and rejection, in the Blake worldview, the penalty of experience. (This poem is from the *Songs of Experience*, which contrast sharply with Blake's *Songs of Innocence*.) The use of symbolism extends and enriches the meaning of the poem.

Jonathan Swift, "A Modest Proposal"
For preventing the children of poor people in Ireland, from being a burden on their parents or country, and for making them beneficial to the publick.

1. Most people are surprised and shocked by this essay, so it is important to help students understand that it is satire and that Swift uses irony to say one thing and mean quite the opposite. As background, it helps to know that Swift had made many sensible proposals for alleviating the poverty of Ireland, to no avail. With this essay, he used satire to propose something horrifying and outrageous to bring attention to his cause. We know that his "proposal" is ironic because it is unthinkable. The narrator speaks in a clear, reasoned voice: logical (*whoever could find out a fair, cheap and easy method of making these children sound and useful members of the common-wealth, would deserve so well of the publick, as to have his statue set up for a preserver of the nation*), detailed (*a young healthy child well nursed, is, at a year old, a most delicious nourishing*

and wholesome food, whether stewed, roasted, baked, or boiled; and I make no doubt that it will equally serve in a fricasie, or a ragoust), and rational (*I shall now therefore humbly propose my own thoughts, which I hope will not be liable to the least objection.*). But his proposal is so shocking and terrifying that, juxtaposed to Swift's actual proposals later in the essay (in the final two paragraphs of this passage), the perceptive reader clearly understands that it is irony.

2. Swift uses irony for its shock value, to draw attention to his cause. Sometimes irony is humorous, but in this essay, Swift uses the sharp pen of satire rather than light humor to criticize the treatment of the poor and disadvantaged. The implication is that the rich might as well eat the poor since they are already making it impossible for the poor to live. Swift's straightforward and actual proposals (described in the final two paragraphs of this passage) were ignored during his time. He stresses this when he says ironically *Therefore let no man talk to me of other expedients.*

President John F. Kennedy, Inaugural Address

1. President Kennedy uses metonymy in the first sentence when he says, *only a few generations have been granted the role of defending freedom in its hour of maximum danger.* A generation cannot have a role in defending freedom. It is the *people* of a particular time, and assuredly not all of the people, that have this responsibility. Kennedy uses something closely related for what he actually means. By using metonymy, Kennedy includes all Americans. Metonymy underscores the importance of defending freedom, and its use enhances the meaning of his speech.

2. Kennedy uses light imagery in the last sentence of this passage. *We see* our country and those who serve aglow with *energy, faith, and devotion.* The image is intensified by calling the light a fire *that can truly light the world.* The visual experience is clear and profound. *Light* is also the figurative term of a metaphor. The literal term is implied; it is the results of the energy, faith, and devotion, the power to bring goodwill and freedom to our country and the world. This power does not literally light anything. It is not a literal fire. But it is *like* a light and a fire: It brings the country and the world out of the darkness of evil, and it can spread freedom throughout the world, like fire. *Light* is also a symbol, a traditional symbol of truth, knowledge, and hope. In its symbolic value, it *is* a light, illuminating and clarifying; but it is also something else: truth, knowledge, and hope. Kennedy evokes that symbolic value of light as he inspires his listeners to defend freedom.

William Shakespeare, Sonnet 116, *The Works of Shakespeare*

1. The chart on page 45 lists metaphors and personification and their literal and figurative terms in the sonnet.

   All of the figures of speech in the sonnet add beauty, precision, complexity of language, and nuances of meaning to the sonnet. The theme is relatively simple, but the figurative language makes the sonnet ring with passion and truth. Compare it with doggerel like this:

   > True love can never change
   > When troubles are around.
   > I know it must seem strange
   > But to this truth I'm bound.

   It might be fun to let students write a few of these colorless rhymes themselves.

2. The symbol in the sonnet is the star in line 7. It is a symbol because it *is* a star *and* something else, a guide and help for navigation, here love guiding the lovers through the ups and downs that all lovers experience. There are two examples of metonymy. The first is *the marriage of true minds.* Here Shakespeare is, of course, talking about the marriage of two faithful people. His use of *two minds* (metonymy, the use of something closely related to what is meant to bring freshness and depth to the meaning) stresses the importance of commitment that transcends the physical and is not subject to change. The second metonym, *rosy lips and cheeks*, are an aspect of youth. Here they represent ephemeral qualities that *are* subject to time. The figures of speech add beauty and depth of meaning, and they help the reader to understand the sonnet on many different levels.

Figure of Speech	Type	Literal Term	Figurative Term
Bends with the remover to remove	personification	love that is not love	a person who is inconstant when circumstances change
It is an ever-fixèd mark, *That looks on tempests, and is never shaken*	metaphor	love	*an ever-fixèd mark* (like a star) *that looks on tempests, and is never shaken*
Tempests	metaphor	life's troubles (implied)	tempests
It is the star to every wandering bark	metaphor	star bark (boat)	love lover
Time	personification	passing of time	the grim reaper with his sickle
Love's not Time's fool	personification	love	time's fool (someone who is duped by time)

Imagery

Consider:

The many men, so beautiful!
And they all dead did lie:
And a thousand thousand slimy things
Lived on; and so did I.

. . . .

Within the shadow of the ship
I watched their rich attire:
Blue, glossy green, and velvet black,
They coiled and swam; and every track
Was a flash of golden fire.

Samuel Taylor Coleridge, "The Rime of the Ancient Mariner"

Discuss:

1. These stanzas from "The Rime of the Ancient Mariner" show the Mariner's changing attitude toward the creatures of the sea. What is the Mariner's attitude in the first stanza? What image reveals this attitude?

2. What is the Mariner's attitude in the second stanza? Analyze the imagery that reveals this change.

Apply:

Think of a cat or a dog you can describe easily. First, write a description that reveals a positive attitude toward the animal. Then think of the same animal and write a description that reveals a negative attitude. Remember, the animal's looks do not change; only your attitude changes. Use imagery rather than explanation to create your descriptions.

Imagery

Consider:

She looked into the distance, and the old terror flamed up for an instant, then sank again. Edna heard her father's voice and her sister Margaret's. She heard the barking of an old dog that was chained to the sycamore tree. The spurs of the cavalry officer clanged as he walked across the porch. There was the hum of bees, and the musky odor of pinks filled the air.

Kate Chopin, *The Awakening*

Discuss:

1. Although the main character, Edna, looks *into the distance*, the images are primarily auditory. What are the auditory images in the passage? What mood do these images create?

2. The last sentence of this passage contains an olfactory image (*the musky odor of pinks filled the air*). What effect does the use of an olfactory image, after a series of auditory images, have on the reader?

Apply:

Write a paragraph in which you create a scene through auditory imagery. The purpose of your paragraph is to create a calm, peaceful mood. Use one olfactory image at the end of your paragraph to enhance the mood created by auditory imagery.

Imagery

Consider:

I sat on the stump of a tree at his feet, and below us stretched the land, the great expanse of the forests, sombre under the sunshine, rolling like a sea, with glints of winding rivers, the grey spots of villages, and here and there a clearing, like an islet of light amongst the dark waves of continuous tree-tops. A brooding gloom lay over this vast and monotonous landscape; the light fell on it as if into an abyss. The land devoured the sunshine; only far off, along the coast, the empty ocean, smooth and polished within the faint haze, seemed to rise up to the sky in a wall of steel.

Joseph Conrad, *Lord Jim*

Discuss:

1. Fill out the chart below with images from the passage:

Images of Land	Images of Sea

2. What attitude toward the land and the sea do these images convey?

Apply:

Select a partner and describe an utterly silent experience you have had. Your partner should write down one visual (and nonfigurative) image from your description. Switch with your partner and repeat the procedure. Share the images with the class.

Imagery

Consider:

Queen: There is a willow grows aslant a brook,
That shows his hoar* leaves in the glassy stream.   *gray or white
There with fantastic garlands did she come
Of crow-flowers, nettles, daisies, and long purples . . .
There, on the pendent boughs her coronet weeds   (5)
Clambering to hang, an envious sliver broke;
When down her weedy trophies and herself
Fell in the weeping brook. Her clothes spread wide,
And, mermaid-like, awhile they bore her up;
Which time she chanted snatches of old tunes,   (10)
As one incapable of* her own distress,   *insensible to
Or like a creature native and indued*   *endowed
Unto that element: but long it could not be
Till that her garments, heavy with their drink,
Pull'd the poor wretch from her melodious lay   (15)
To muddy death.

William Shakespeare, *Hamlet*

Discuss:

1. This play explores several themes: madness, loyalty, love, and revenge. In this passage, Hamlet's mother (the queen) is describing Hamlet's girlfriend (Ophelia) and her descent into madness and death. Examine lines 8–13. How does the imagery in these lines help the reader understand Ophelia's madness?

2. Line 10 is not figurative. Would it strengthen or weaken the line to change the image to a simile such as *Which time she sang like a flawed recording*? Defend your opinion.

Apply:

Write an image that captures a moment of intense exuberance. Your image should be no more than one sentence and should contain no figurative language. Share your image with the class.

Imagery

Consider:

As for the grass, it grew as scant as hair
In leprosy; thin dry blades prick'd the mud
Which underneath look'd kneaded up with blood.
One stiff blind horse, his every bone a-stare,
Stood stupefied, however he came there:
Thrust out past service from the devil's stud!

Robert Browning, "Childe Roland to the Dark Tower Came"

Discuss:

1. What feelings are produced by the image of the grass in lines 1–3?

2. Does the imagery of the horse (lines 4–6) inspire sympathy? Explain your answer with direct references to specific images.

Apply:

Write a description of an old, sick animal. Convey an attitude of horror through the imagery of your description. Do not explain the sense of horror; do not use figurative language. Instead, use specific imagery to convey the meaning of your description. Share your description with the class.

Discussion Suggestions
Imagery

Samuel Taylor Coleridge, "The Rime of the Ancient Mariner"

1. The Mariner's attitude in the first stanza is revealed through the contrasting imagery associated with the men and the creatures of the sea. The dead men are described as *beautiful*. In contrast, the creatures of the sea are seen as inferior to men, not worthy of living. The image that reveals the attitude about the sea creatures is the *thousand thousand slimy things* that live on even though the men have died. The creatures of the sea are not even named. The persona calls them *slimy things*, which diminishes their importance. They are also linked with the narrator (*a thousand thousand slimy things / Lived on; and so did I...*), who is reviled at this point in the poem; and they share the narrator's virulence.

2. In the second stanza, the Mariner completely changes his attitude toward the sea creatures. They are no longer *a thousand thousand slimy things*; instead, they have a *rich attire*. The colors used to describe the creatures are specific and positive. The green is *glossy*; the black is *velvet*. They leave a *track of golden fire* as they *coil* and *swim*. The sea creatures are no longer seen as vile; rather, they are resplendent and beautiful.

Kate Chopin, *The Awakening*

1. Auditory images include her father's voice, her sister Margaret's voice, the barking of a dog, the spurs of a cavalry officer, and the hum of bees. These images create a mood of loneliness. All of the images of ordinary life are in the distance, audible but not immediate. Nothing directly interacts with Edna. She is a watcher and a listener, removed from the homely action of the passage.

2. The olfactory image brings the reader back to Edna. The auditory images are all in the distance. However, the olfactory image *fill[s] the air*. It shifts the reader's attention and concern back to Edna and her loneliness.

Joseph Conrad, *Lord Jim*

1. The chart should include the following:

Images of the Land	Images of the Sea
the stump of a tree *the great expanse of the forests* *forests, sombre under the sunshine* *forests, rolling like a sea* *glints of winding rivers* *grey spots of villages* *a clearing, like an islet of light amongst the dark waves of continuous tree-tops* *a brooding gloom . . . over this vast and monotonous landscape* *the land devoured the sunshine*	*the empty ocean, smooth and polished within the faint haze, seemed to rise up to the sky in a wall of steel*

2. All of the descriptive power of this passage is bound to images of the sea. Most of the images of the land are dark and monotonous: *the great expanse of the forests; forests, sombre under the sunshine; grey spots of villages; a brooding gloom; the land devoured the sunshine.* The only active images of the land refer to the sea or water: *forests, rolling like a sea; the glints of winding rivers; and a clearing, like an islet of light amongst the dark waves of continuous tree-tops.* The land is gloomy, inactive, and full of foreboding. The sea, on the other hand, *is smooth and polished and rises up to the sky in a wall of steel.* The ocean is an actor, an equal participant with the sky. It rises on its own, generating its own strength; and its power is prodigious: *a wall of steel.* The attitude conveyed is that the land is to be endured. The sea, however, is to be celebrated; for in the sea lies life and power.

William Shakespeare, *Hamlet*

1. The imagery shows Ophelia's madness by revealing that she does nothing to save herself from drowning. She is kept afloat only by her clothes (*Her clothes spread wide, / And, mermaid-like, awhile they bore her*

up). She sings songs as she floats, buoyed up by her clothes, certain to drown (*Which time she chanted snatches of old tunes*). And she is totally oblivious to her own danger (*As one incapable of her own distress / Or like a creature native and indued / Unto that element*).

2. The plaintive simplicity of the line—the image of Ophelia singing as she drowns—makes no judgment. Therein lies its strength. The image captures and reflects her innocence and her oblivion to her own impending doom.

Robert Browning, "Childe Roland to the Dark Tower Came"

1. The image produces feelings of horror and disgust. The grass is sparse, so sparse that there are only *thin dry blades*, indicating barrenness and dissipation. Further, the grass is compared to hair in leprosy. The association with leprosy (in Browning's time) suggests people with skin rotting off their bodies, excluded from the company of others. This association is compounded by the image of the mud *kneaded up with blood*. The imagery's total effect is one of revulsion and horror.

2. The imagery of the horse in lines 4–6 does not inspire sympathy. While it is true that his looks are pathetic (*One stiff blind horse, his every bone a-stare*), the rest of the imagery does not produce a sympathetic reaction. The horse is *stupefied*, dull and lacking animation. This image is in keeping with the *thin dry blades* of line 2 and indicates waste and dissolution. The final image of the passage removes what sympathy the reader might still have. This image (*Thrust out past service from the devil's stud!*) reveals that the horse comes from a world of evil. He is past service now, but his work was engendering evil, and his ruin springs from his work.

Syntax

Consider:

Brother, continue to listen.

You say that you are sent to instruct us how to worship the Great Spirit agreeably to his mind, and, if we do not take hold of the religion which you white people teach, we shall be unhappy hereafter. You say that you are right and we are lost. How do we know this to be true?

> Seneca Chief Red Jacket, "Indian Speech, Delivered Before a Gentleman Missionary, from Massachusetts, by a Chief, Commonly Called by the White People Red Jacket. His Indian Name Is Sagu-ya-what-hath, Which Being Interpreted, Is Keeper-Awake"

Discuss:

1. The words *you say* are repeated several times in the sentence. What is the repetition's function?

2. The question at the end of the passage is a rhetorical question. What attitude toward the audience is expressed by the use of a rhetorical question?

Apply:

Write a three-sentence paragraph modeled after the passage by Sagu-ya-what-hath. The first two sentences should contain repetition; the third sentence should be a rhetorical question. Your topic is school uniforms. Share your paragraph with the class.

Syntax

Consider:

I hear an army charging upon the land,

And the thunder of horses plunging, foam about their knees:

Arrogant, in black armor, behind them stand,

Disdaining the reins, with fluttering whips, the charioteers.

James Joyce, "I Hear an Army"

Discuss:

1. The subject of the verb *stand* in line 3 is *charioteers* at the end of line 4. How does this inversion of the normal word order (subject-verb) affect the impact of those lines?

2. Examine the adjectives and adjective phrases (*arrogant, in black armor*) in lines 3 and 4. What word do these adjectives modify? How does this unusual word order affect the impact of the lines?

Apply:

Write a sentence about a bicycle crash. In your sentence invert the normal order of subject and verb. Try to make your sentence sound natural and powerful. Share your sentence with a partner.

Syntax

Consider:

He slowly ventured into the pond. The bottom was deep, soft clay, he sank in, and the water clasped dead cold round his legs.

D. H. Lawrence, "The Horse-Dealer's Daughter," *England, My England, and Other Stories*

Discuss:

1. What effect does sentence length have on this passage?

2. Examine the second sentence. How does the structure of the sentence reinforce the meaning?

Apply:

Write a sentence in which you make an inanimate object active by using an active verb. Remember that your verb is not just an action verb (like *talk* or *flow*). The verb must make your inanimate object into an actor, a doer. Share your sentence with the class.

Syntax

Consider:

Death be not proud, though some have called thee

Mighty and dreadful, for, thou art not soe;

For those whom thou think'st thou dost overthrow

Die not, poore Death; nor yet canst thou kill me.

From rest and sleep, which but thy pictures bee,

Much pleasure, then from thee much more must flow;

John Donne, "Death Be Not Proud"

Note: John Donne, a British poet who lived in the 16th and 17th centuries, used some spellings that we no longer use. In this selection, *soe* is an old spelling of *so*, *poore* of *poor*, and *bee* of *be*.

Discuss:

1. This poem is an expression of the poet's strong faith in religion and the promise of an afterlife. This faith underlies the structure of the poem. What is the effect of opening the first sentence with the imperative mood (expressing a command) of the verb *to be*?

2. In the first clause of the second sentence (lines 5–6), the verb is understood; in the second clause of this sentence, the subject is understood. What verb is omitted? What subject is omitted? What effect does this have on the meaning of the lines?

Apply:

Write a sentence about smartphones. Begin your sentence with a verb in the imperative mood (expressing a command), as in line 1 of Donne's poem. Share your sentence with a partner and discuss the attitude toward smartphones that your opening verb reveals.

Syntax

Consider:

While we do these things, these deeply momentous things, let us be very clear, and make very clear to all the world, what our motives and our objects are.

President Woodrow Wilson, Address to Congress Requesting a Declaration of War Against Germany

Discuss:

1. This is a periodic sentence, one in which the main subject and verb are delayed until the final part of the sentence. This creates syntactic tension and emphasizes the ideas at the end of the sentence. What ideas are stressed in this periodic sentence?

2. How would it change the effectiveness of the sentence if we rewrote it as follows?

   Our motives and objects must be clear to all the world
   while we do these deeply momentous things.

Apply:

Using President Wilson's sentence as a model, write a periodic sentence about music censorship. Read your sentence to the class and explain how the syntax of your sentence affects the meaning.

Discussion Suggestions
Syntax

Seneca Chief Red Jacket, "Indian Speech, Delivered Before a Gentleman Missionary, from Massachusetts, by a Chief, Commonly Called by the White People Red Jacket. His Indian Name Is Sagu-ya-what-hath, Which Being Interpreted, Is Keeper-Awake"

1. Sagu-ya-what-hath repeats the words *you say* to mark a refutation and to emphasize the words. Everything that follows the *you say* is denied. The conscious repetition of a word or phrase at the beginning of several successive verses, clauses, or paragraphs is called anaphora. Functions of anaphora vary: emphasis, irony, and/or refutation of what follows.

2. A rhetorical question is one for which no answer is expected. The answer is assumed. In this case the answer is obvious: We cannot *know this to be true.* The rhetorical question reinforces the refutation of the anaphora and conveys a clear feeling of mistrust for the audience.

James Joyce, "I Hear an Army"

1. Inversion of normal word order shocks or surprises the reader and emphasizes the inverted words of the sentence. The inversion here also delays syntactic closure, increasing the tension of the sentence and holding the reader's attention until the sentence is complete.

2. *Arrogant* and *in black armor* modify *charioteers.* The unusual word order heightens and directs the reader's attentiveness. The word order forces the reader to examine the line closely in order to determine the subject and holds the reader's attention until the end of the fourth line.

D. H. Lawrence, "The Horse-Dealer's Daughter," *England, My England, and Other Stories*

1. This passage has a short sentence followed by a much longer one. The introductory, short sentence states the main idea of the passage. It is simple, straightforward prose and prepares the reader for the descriptive sentence that follows. The longer sentence amplifies the first sentence, developing and expanding its ideas (the pond, his venturing into the pond).

2. The structure of this sentence is convoluted and irregular. The clause *he sank in* seems out of place syntactically. (Does it modify *bottom*? Is it adverbial? Is it a misprint?) But the sentence works because its structure reflects its meaning. He sinks into the pond as we sink into the sentence. The form of the sentence is as amorphous as the soft clay and the clasping water.

John Donne, "Death Be Not Proud"

1. The imperative mood is used for commands and advice. When the persona tells Death to *be not proud*, he is demonstrating his own power and control. Death cannot conquer the persona in this poem because he firmly believes he can surmount death because of his religion. The effect of the imperative is to startle the reader and emphasize the power of faith.

2. The understood verb is *must flow*, and the understood subject is *pleasure*. By leaving out words in the first clause that are stated in the second clause (and vice versa), Donne connects the ideas of the two clauses. His syntax reflects his meaning: We get pleasure from rest and sleep. Rest and sleep are only reflections of death. Therefore, we will get even more pleasure from death than from rest and sleep, due to the promise of salvation.

President Woodrow Wilson, Address to Congress Requesting a Declaration of War Against Germany

1. President Wilson stresses, by using this periodic sentence, that our motives and objects must be clear.

2. The new sentence reduces the syntactic tension, diminishes the interest of the sentence, and changes the focus of the sentence. The stress is no longer on the *motives and objects*. Instead, it is on the *deeply momentous things*.

Tone

Consider:

But that is Cooper's way; frequently he will explain and justify little things that do not need it and then make up for this by as frequently failing to explain important ones that do need it. For instance he allowed that astute and cautious person, Deerslayer-Hawkeye, to throw his rifle heedlessly down and leave it lying on the ground where some hostile Indians would presently be sure to find it—a rifle prized by that person above all things else in the earth—and the reader gets no word of explanation of that strange act. There was a reason, but it wouldn't bear exposure. Cooper meant to get a fine dramatic effect out of the finding of the rifle by the Indians, and he accomplished this at the happy time; but all the same, Hawkeye could have hidden the rifle in a quarter of a minute where the Indians could not have found it. Cooper couldn't think of any way to explain why Hawkeye didn't do that, so he just shirked the difficulty and did not explain at all.

Mark Twain, "Fenimore Cooper's Further Literary Offences"

Discuss:

1. This essay is Twain's analysis of James Fenimore Cooper's writing style. What is Twain's tone in this passage? What is central to the tone of this passage: the attitude toward the speaker, the subject, or the reader?

2. How does Twain create the tone?

Apply:

Write a paragraph about a movie you have recently seen. Create a critical, disparaging tone through your choice of details. Use Twain's paragraph as a model. Share your paragraph with the class.

Tone

Consider:

The best part of human language, properly so called, is derived from reflection on the acts of the mind itself. It is formed by a voluntary appropriation of fixed symbols to internal acts, to processes and results of imagination, the greater part of which have no place in the consciousness of uneducated man; though in civilized society, by imitation and passive remembrance of what they hear from their religious instructors and other superiors, the most uneducated share in the harvest which they neither sowed nor reaped.

Samuel Taylor Coleridge, *Biographia Literaria*

Discuss:

1. What is Coleridge's attitude toward the uneducated man?

2. How does Coleridge's choice of details, diction, and syntax reveal his attitude toward the uneducated man?

Apply:

Rewrite the first sentence of this passage. Keep the same basic ideas that Coleridge expresses, but change the tone. Your tone should express contempt for academic elitism. Choose details, diction, and syntax that support your tone. Share your sentence with the class.

Tone

Consider:

In Pride, in reasoning Pride, our error lies;
All quit their sphere, and rush into the skies.
Pride still is aiming at the best abodes,
Men would be Angels, Angels would be Gods.
Aspiring to be Gods, if Angels fell,
Aspiring to be Angels, Men rebel:
And who but wishes to invert the laws
Of Order, sins against th' Eternal Cause.

Alexander Pope, "An Essay on Man"

Discuss:

1. What is Pope's attitude toward pride, the subject matter? Cite your evidence.

2. What is the tone of this passage? What attitude underlies the tone?

Apply:

Write a short paragraph of advice about texting in class. Show through your diction and choice of detail that you believe yourself superior in every way to your reader. **Never directly state your superiority. Instead, let the tone of your paragraph carry your haughty attitude.**

Tone

Consider:

JACK *(slowly and hesitantly):* Gwendolen—Cecily—it is very painful for me to be forced to speak the truth. It is the first time in my life that I have ever been reduced to such a painful position, and I am really quite inexperienced in doing anything of the kind. However I will tell you quite frankly that I have no brother Ernest. I have no brother at all. I never had a brother in my life, and I certainly have not the smallest intention of ever having one in the future.

Oscar Wilde, *The Importance of Being Earnest*

Discuss:

1. What is Wilde's attitude toward Jack? What specific diction and detail reveal this attitude?

2. What is Wilde's attitude toward the reader? How do you know?

Apply:

Rewrite Jack's lines to reflect the attitude that lying is terribly wrong. Adopt a disdainful attitude toward your audience and a scornful attitude toward Jack. Share your lines with the class.

Tone

Consider:

. . . The gracious Duncan
Was pitied of Macbeth:—marry, he was dead:—
And the right-valiant Banquo walkt too late;
Whom, you may say, if't please you, Fleance kill'd,
For Fleance fled: men must not walk too late.   (5)
Who <u>cannot want the thought</u>,* how monstrous   *can avoid thinking
It was for Malcolm and for Donalbain
To kill their gracious father? damned fact*!   *deed
How it did grieve Macbeth! did he not straight,
In pious rage, the two delinquents tear,   (10)
That were the slaves of drink and thralls* of sleep?   *slaves
Was not that nobly done? Ay, and wisely too;
For 'twould have anger'd any heart alive
To hear the men deny't. So that, I say,
He has <u>borne</u>* all things well; and I do think   (15)   *carried off
That, had he Duncan's sons under his key,—
As, <u>an't</u>* please heaven, he shall not,—they should find   *if it
What 'twere to kill a father; so should Fleance.

William Shakespeare, *Macbeth*

Discuss:

1. The speaker in this passage is a lord in Macbeth's court. His attitude is critical of Macbeth, but his tone is not critical, angry, or vengeful. How would you characterize the tone of this passage? Defend your views.

2. Shakespeare uses the simple image of a man walking in lines 3 and 5. How does this image contribute to the tone of the passage?

Apply:

Write a paragraph that, in a direct and angry manner, states that Macbeth is a tyrant who killed Duncan and Banquo to gain power. Read your paragraph to the class and discuss the effect this change in tone has on a reader.

Discussion Suggestions
Tone

Mark Twain, "Fenimore Cooper's Further Literary Offences"

1. Twain's tone in this passage is contemptuous and sarcastic. Central to the tone is Twain's attitude toward the subject: Cooper's writing, which he finds inconsistent and irresponsible.

2. Twain creates his tone through diction and selection of detail. He criticizes Cooper and states, *But that is Cooper's way*, generalizing the criticism. He accuses Cooper of *shirk[ing]* difficulties in writing. He calls Hawkeye that *astute and cautious person*, then shows him to be *heedless*. Through detail he contrasts Hawkeye's reputation as a character (*astute* and *cautious*) with Hawkeye's careless actions: *Hawkeye, throw[s] his rifle heedlessly down and leave[s] it lying on the ground where some hostile Indians would presently be sure to find it—a rifle prized by that person above all things else in the earth*. He supports the contrast with the contention that the carelessness has no cogent motivation: *Hawkeye could have hidden the rifle in a quarter of a minute where the Indians could not have found it*. Further, Twain's contempt for Cooper's writing is underscored by direct criticism of Cooper's style. He states: *frequently he will explain and justify little things that do not need it and then make up for this by as frequently failing to explain important ones that do need it* and *Cooper couldn't think of any way to explain why Hawkeye didn't do that, so he just shirked the difficulty and did not explain at all*.

Samuel Taylor Coleridge, *Biographia Literaria*

1. Coleridge's attitude toward the uneducated man is condescending and patronizing.

2. Coleridge states that uneducated men are neither capable of reflection on thought nor of participation in acts of the imagination. They can only benefit from association with educated men. This is clearly supported by details, diction, and syntax. The *best part of human language* has *no place in the consciousness of uneducated man*. Coleridge calls educated men *superiors* and states that uneducated men can participate in the life of the mind only *by imitation and passive remembrance of what they hear from their religious instructors and other superiors*. Further, he calls this participation a *harvest which they neither sowed nor reaped*. The syntax of the second sentence also reveals Coleridge's attitude toward the uneducated man. The sentence is composed of two long clauses connected by a semicolon. The first clause is an independent clause (*it is formed*), which carries the weight and focus of the sentence (the educated man). The second clause is a subordinate clause (*the most uneducated share*), which underscores the dependency of the uneducated on the educated. The two clauses are joined by a semicolon, reiterating the close connection between the educated and uneducated man (one learns by *imitation and passive remembrance* from the other).

Alexander Pope, "An Essay on Man"

1. Pope's attitude toward pride, typical of neoclassical writing, is that there is a natural order to things; and anyone who tampers with the natural order is guilty of pride. Pride, according to Pope, is the cause of much suffering and evil in the world. He states this simply in the first line of the passage: *In Pride, in reasoning Pride, our error lies*. He compares the pride of men to the pride of angels with the intent of stressing the dangers of perverting what Pope believes is the natural order of things: *Aspiring to be Gods, if Angels fell, / Aspiring to be Angels, Men rebel*. Pope furthers his argument by comparing Satan's fall from grace (when he rebelled against God) to man's fall to his ruin if he gives in to pride: *And who but wishes to invert the laws / Of Order, sins against th' Eternal Cause*.

2. The tone of this passage is didactic. In other words, the intent of the passage is to instruct. The attitude that underlies the tone is the attitude toward the reader, his audience. Pope assumes a superiority and views the reader as one needing instruction and edification. That is why Pope's writing often sounds preachy. He emphasizes words with capital letters and speaks with great authority and certainty: *In Pride, in reasoning Pride, our error lies*. And he assumes an absolute knowledge of God's plan: *who but wishes to invert the laws/Of Order, sins against th' Eternal Cause*. Tone can be shaped by the author's (or narrator's) attitude toward subject matter, the audience, or both. Here tone is determined mainly by the author's attitude toward his audience.

Oscar Wilde, *The Importance of Being Earnest*

1. Wilde characterizes Jack as a frivolous, silly man with weak morals. It is *painful* for him *to speak the truth*. It is the first time in his life that he has spoken the truth, and it hurts him to do so. Further, his reference to having a brother (*I certainly have not the smallest intention of ever having one in the future*) as if it were in his control underscores his shallow pretentiousness.

2. Wilde's tone is satirical: He mocks Jack and his whole world of superficial, pretentious compatriots. His attitude toward the reader—conspiratorial and concurrent—sets the tone. Wilde assumes an audience in concord. Jack's seriously delivered lines (*. . . it is very painful for me to be forced to speak the truth. It is the first time in my life that I have ever been reduced to such a painful position, and I am really quite inexperienced in doing anything of the kind*) would fall flat without an audience that 1) recognizes the familiarity of people like Jack; 2) sees the comic potential of someone who admits to putting pretense and the appearance of virtue over real virtue; and 3) recognizes the ironic honesty of stating truthfully the preference for pretense over truth. The interplay of attitudes toward the subject and the audience accounts for the humor of the passage, creates the satire, and sets the tone of the passage.

William Shakespeare, *Macbeth*

1. The tone of this passage is ironic. The speaker says one thing—that Macbeth is pious and honest—and means quite another—that Macbeth is ruthless and cruel. The key to the irony of the passage is in line 17, the reference to Macbeth's possible capture of Duncan's sons, Malcolm and Donalbain. The speaker says parenthetically: *As, an't please heaven, he shall not.* This line is not ironic; it reveals the speaker's true attitude: He fears Macbeth and hopes Donalbain and Malcolm will not fall under his power. The speaker uses diction, detail, and imagery to reinforce the irony of the rest of the passage. He says *the gracious Duncan/ Was pitied of Macbeth*, but Macbeth killed Duncan. Malcolm and Donalbain flee after their father's murder and are implicated in the murder. The speaker shows the absurdity of this by comparing Fleance's flight from his father's murderers to Malcolm and Donalbain's flight and saying ironically that Fleance probably murdered his father, too: *right-valiant Banquo walkt too late; / Whom, you may say, if't please you, Fleance killed, / For Fleance fled.* The speaker also describes Macbeth's killing of the guards, the only possible witnesses to the murder, *in pious rage.* We know this is ironic, because the speaker says it was *wisely* done by Macbeth, implying that it would have been unwise to let the guards live, that they could have incriminated Macbeth. Further, Macbeth has *borne all things well*, diction that reveals Macbeth had a plan.

2. The image of a man walking late at night is innocent and benign. Yet the speaker refers to it as if it were the cause of the murders (*Banquo walkt too late . . . men must not walk too late*). The image reinforces the ironic tone of the passage by making the trivial (*walking too late*) important and making the important (the ruthless murders) trivial.

Developing Voice

Katherine Mansfield,
"A Dill Pickle," *Bliss and Other Stories*

AND then, after six years, she saw him again. He was seated at one of those little bamboo tables decorated with a Japanese vase of paper daffodils. There was a tall plate of fruit in front of him, and very carefully, in a way she recognized immediately as his "special" way, he was peeling an orange.

He must have felt that shock of recognition in her for he looked up and met her eyes. Incredible! He didn't know her! She smiled; he frowned. She came towards him. He closed his eyes an instant, but opening them his face lit up as though he had struck a match in a dark room. He laid down the orange and pushed back his chair, and she took her little warm hand out of her muff and gave it to him.

"Vera!" he exclaimed. "How strange. Really, for a moment I didn't know you. Won't you sit down? You've had lunch? Won't you have some coffee?"

She hesitated, but of course she meant to.

"Yes, I'd like some coffee." And she sat down opposite him.

"You've changed. You've changed very much," he said, staring at her with that eager, lighted look. "You look so well. I've never seen you look so well before."

"Really?" She raised her veil and unbuttoned her high fur collar. "I don't feel very well. I can't bear this weather, you know."

"Ah, no. You hate the cold. . . ."

"Loathe it." She shuddered. "And the worst of it is that the older one grows . . ."

He interrupted her. "Excuse me," and tapped on the table for the waitress. "Please bring some coffee and cream." To her: "You are sure you won't eat anything? Some fruit, perhaps. The fruit here is very good."

"No, thanks. Nothing."

"Then that's settled." And smiling just a hint too broadly he took up the orange again. "You were saying—the older one grows—"

"The colder," she laughed. But she was thinking how well she remembered that trick of his—the trick of interrupting her—and of how it used to exasperate her six years ago. She used to feel then as though he, quite suddenly, in the middle of what she was saying, put his hand over her lips, turned from her, attended to something different, and then took his hand away, and with just the same slightly too broad smile, gave her his attention again. . . . Now we are ready. That is settled.

"The colder!" He echoed her words, laughing too. "Ah, ah. You still say the same things. And there is another thing about you that is not changed at all—your beautiful voice—your beautiful way of speaking." Now he was very grave; he leaned towards her, and she smelled the warm, stinging scent of the orange peel. "You have only to say one word and I would know your voice among all other voices. I don't know what it is—I've often wondered—that makes your voice such a—haunting memory. . . . Do you remember that first afternoon we spent together at Kew Gardens? You were so surprised because I did not know the names of any flowers. I am still just as ignorant for all your telling me. But whenever it is very fine and warm, and I see some bright colours—it's awfully strange—I hear your voice saying: 'Geranium, marigold and verbena.' And I feel those three words are all I recall of some forgotten, heavenly language. . . . You remember that afternoon?"

"Oh, yes, very well." She drew a long, soft breath, as though the paper daffodils between them were almost too sweet to bear. Yet, what had remained in her mind of that particular afternoon was an absurd scene over the tea table. A great many people taking tea in a Chinese pagoda, and he behaving like a maniac about the wasps—waving them away, flapping at them with his straw hat, serious and infuriated out of all proportion to the occasion. How delighted the sniggering tea drinkers had been. And how she had suffered.

But now, as he spoke, that memory faded. His was the truer. Yes, it had been a wonderful afternoon, full of geranium and marigold and verbena, and—warm sunshine. Her thoughts lingered over the last two words as though she sang them.

In the warmth, as it were, another memory unfolded. She saw herself sitting on a lawn. He lay beside her, and suddenly, after a long silence, he rolled over and put his head in her lap.

"I wish," he said, in a low, troubled voice, "I wish that I had taken poison and were about to die—here now!"

At that moment a little girl in a white dress, holding a long, dripping water lily, dodged from behind a bush, stared at them, and dodged back again. But he did not see. She leaned over him.

"Ah, why do you say that? I could not say that."

But he gave a kind of soft moan, and taking her hand he held it to his cheek.

"Because I know I am going to love you too much—far too much. And I shall suffer so terribly, Vera, because you never, never will love me."

He was certainly far better looking now than he had been then. He had lost all that dreamy vagueness and indecision. Now he had the air of a man who has found his place in life, and fills it with a confidence and an assurance which was, to say the least, impressive. He must have made money, too. His clothes were admirable, and at that moment he pulled a Russian cigarette case out of his pocket.

"Won't you smoke?"

"Yes, I will." She hovered over them. "They look very good."

"I think they are. I get them made for me by a little man in St. James's Street. I don't smoke very much. I'm not like you—but when I do, they must be delicious, very fresh cigarettes.

Smoking isn't a habit with me; it's a luxury—like perfume. Are you still so fond of perfumes? Ah, when I was in Russia . . ."

She broke in: "You've really been to Russia?"

"Oh, yes. I was there for over a year. Have you forgotten how we used to talk of going there?"

"No, I've not forgotten."

He gave a strange half laugh and leaned back in his chair. "Isn't it curious. I have really carried out all those journeys that we planned. Yes, I have been to all those places that we talked of, and stayed in them long enough to—as you used to say, 'air oneself' in them. In fact, I have spent the last three years of my life travelling all the time. Spain, Corsica, Siberia, Russia, Egypt. The only country left is China, and I mean to go there, too, when the war is over."

As he spoke, so lightly, tapping the end of his cigarette against the ash-tray, she felt the strange beast that had slumbered so long within her bosom stir, stretch itself, yawn, prick up its ears, and suddenly bound to its feet, and fix its longing, hungry stare upon those far away places. But all she said was, smiling gently: "How I envy you."

He accepted that. "It has been," he said, "very wonderful—especially Russia. Russia was all that we had imagined, and far, far more. I even spent some days on a river boat on the Volga. Do you remember that boatman's song that you used to play?"

"Yes." It began to play in her mind as she spoke.

"Do you ever play it now?"

"No, I've no piano."

He was amazed at that. "But what has become of your beautiful piano?"

She made a little grimace. "Sold. Ages ago."

"But you were so fond of music," he wondered.

"I've no time for it now," said she.

He let it go at that. "That river life," he went on, "is something quite special. After a day or two you cannot realize that you have ever known another. And it is not necessary to know the language—the life of the boat creates a bond between you and the people that's more than sufficient. You eat with them, pass the day with them, and in the evening there is that endless singing."

She shivered, hearing the boatman's song break out again loud and tragic, and seeing the boat floating on the darkening river with melancholy trees on either side. . . . "Yes, I should like that," said she, stroking her muff.

"You'd like almost everything about Russian life," he said warmly. "It's so informal, so impulsive, so free without question. And then the peasants are so splendid. They are such human beings—yes, that is it. Even the man who drives your carriage has—has some real part in what is happening. I remember the evening a party of us, two friends of mine and the wife of one of them, went for a picnic by the Black Sea. We took supper and champagne and ate and drank on the grass. And while we were eating the coachman came up. 'Have a dill pickle,' he said. He wanted to share with us. That seemed to me so right, so—you know what I mean?"

And she seemed at that moment to be sitting on the grass beside the mysteriously Black Sea, black as velvet, and rippling against the banks in silent, velvet waves. She saw the carriage drawn up to one side of the road, and the little group on the grass, their faces and hands white in the moonlight. She saw the pale dress of the woman outspread and her folded parasol, lying on the grass like a huge pearl crochet hook. Apart from them, with his supper in a cloth on his knees, sat the coachman. "Have a dill pickle," said he, and although she was not certain what a dill pickle was, she saw the greenish glass jar with a red chili like a parrot's beak glimmering through. She sucked in her cheeks; the dill pickle was terribly sour. . . .

"Yes, I know perfectly what you mean," she said.

In the pause that followed they looked at each other. In the past when they had looked at each other like that they had felt such a boundless understanding between them that their souls had, as it were, put their arms round each other and dropped into the same sea, content to be drowned, like mournful lovers. But now, the surprising thing was that it was he who held back. He who said:

"What a marvellous listener you are. When you look at me with those wild eyes I feel that I could tell you things that I would never breathe to another human being."

Was there just a hint of mockery in his voice or was it her fancy? She could not be sure.

"Before I met you," he said, "I had never spoken of myself to anybody. How well I remember one night, the night that I brought you the little Christmas tree, telling you all about my childhood. And of how I was so miserable that I ran away and lived under a cart in our yard for two days without being discovered. And you listened, and your eyes shone, and I felt that you had even made the little Christmas tree listen too, as in a fairy story."

But of that evening she had remembered a little pot of caviare. It had cost seven and sixpence. He could not get over it. Think of it—a tiny jar like that costing seven and sixpence. While she ate it he watched her, delighted and shocked.

"No, really, that is eating money. You could not get seven shillings into a little pot that size. Only think of the profit they must make. . . ." And he had begun some immensely complicated calculations. . . . But now good-bye to the caviare. The Christmas tree was on the table, and the little boy lay under the cart with his head pillowed on the yard dog.

"The dog was called Bosun," she cried delightedly.

But he did not follow. "Which dog? Had you a dog? I don't remember a dog at all."

"No, no. I mean the yard dog when you were a little boy." He laughed and snapped the cigarette case to.

"Was he? Do you know I had forgotten that. It seems such ages ago. I cannot believe that it is only six years. After I had recognized you to-day—I had to take such a leap—I had to take a leap over my whole life to get back to that time. I was such a kid then." He drummed on the table. "I've often thought how I must have bored you. And now I understand so perfectly why you wrote to me as you did—although at the time that letter nearly finished my life. I found it again the other day, and I couldn't help laughing as I read it. It was so clever—such a true picture of me." He glanced up. "You're not going?"

She had buttoned her collar again and drawn down her veil.

"Yes, I am afraid I must," she said, and managed a smile. Now she knew that he had been mocking.

"Ah, no, please," he pleaded. "Don't go just for a moment," and he caught up one of her gloves from the table and clutched at it as if that would hold her. "I see so few people to talk to nowadays, that I have turned into a sort of barbarian," he said. "Have I said something to hurt you?"

"Not a bit," she lied. But as she watched him draw her glove through his fingers, gently, gently, her anger really did die down, and besides, at the moment he looked more like himself of six years ago. . . .

"What I really wanted then," he said softly, "was to be a sort of carpet—to make myself into a sort of carpet for you to walk on so that you need not be hurt by the sharp stones and the mud that you hated so. It was nothing more positive than that—nothing more selfish. Only I did desire, eventually, to turn into a magic carpet and carry you away to all those lands you longed to see."

As he spoke she lifted her head as though she drank something; the strange beast in her bosom began to purr. . . .

"I felt that you were more lonely than anybody else in the world," he went on, "and yet, perhaps, that you were the only person in the world who was really, truly alive. Born out of your time," he murmured, stroking the glove, "fated."

Ah, God! What had she done! How had she dared to throw away her happiness like this. This was the only man who had ever understood her. Was it too late? Could it be too late? *She* was that glove that he held in his fingers. . . .

"And then the fact that you had no friends and never had made friends with people. How I understood that, for neither had I. Is it just the same now?"

"Yes," she breathed. "Just the same. I am as alone as ever."

"So am I," he laughed gently, "just the same."

Suddenly with a quick gesture he handed her back the glove and scraped his chair on the floor. "But what seemed to me so mysterious then is perfectly plain to me now. And to you, too, of course. . . . It simply was that we were such egoists, so self-engrossed, so wrapped up in ourselves that we hadn't a corner in our hearts for anybody else. Do you know," he cried, naive and hearty, and dreadfully like another side of that old self again, "I began studying a Mind System when I was in Russia, and I found that we were not peculiar at all. It's quite a well known form of . . ."

She had gone. He sat there, thunder-struck, astounded beyond words. . . . And then he asked the waitress for his bill.

"But the cream has not been touched," he said. "Please do not charge me for it."

To the Student:

♣ Katherine Mansfield was an early 20th century writer from New Zealand. This story reveals an encounter between a man and a woman who had a close relationship several years before but have gone their separate ways. Notice how Mansfield captures the personalities of the two characters and the nature of their relationship through the skillful use of the elements of voice. As with all serious fiction, the reader should consider elements of fiction (theme, conflict, characterization, plot structure, and point of view) as well as the elements of voice as pathways to meaning.

Tone

Mansfield: Lesson One

Consider:

Read the story several times slowly and carefully. Use underlining or highlighting and marginal notes to call attention to parts of the story that you think are critical to an understanding of the characters, theme, and tone.

Discuss:

1. What is the tone of the story? Consider the attitude of the characters toward each other and the implied attitude of the author toward the characters. How would you describe the author's voice?

2. What is the theme of this story? How does the tone support the theme of the story?

Apply:

Write a description of an encounter with someone that makes you nervous. Create a tone of reluctance and confusion. Don't explain the tone; instead, let your use of diction, imagery, and detail capture your feelings and reveal the tone.

Mansfield: Lesson One

Consider:

She raised her veil and **unbuttoned her high fur collar**. "I don't feel very well. I can't bear this weather, you know."

Discuss:

1. What insight into Vera's character do we get from the words *unbuttoned her high fur collar*?

2. How would the impact of the lines change if Mansfield had written, *She raised her veil and loosened her lace collar*?

Apply:

Write a sentence that uses an active verb to reveal a character's nature. Don't explain; let the action reveal the characteristics you want to stress. Use Mansfield's sentence as a model. Share your sentence with a partner.

Mansfield: Lesson Two

Consider:

He gave a strange **half laugh** and leaned back in his chair. "Isn't it **curious**. I have really carried out all those journeys that we planned. . . ."

Discuss:

1. What is a *half laugh*? How does this diction help the reader understand the man's character?

2. How would it change the reader's understanding of the man's character if he had said, "Isn't it **poetic justice**. I have really carried out all those journeys that we planned. . . ."

Apply:

Write a sentence that uses specific diction to capture a laugh that reveals character. Use Mansfield's sentence as a model. Share your sentence with the class.

Detail

Mansfield: Lesson One

Consider:

"You'd like almost everything about Russian life," he said warmly. "It's so informal, so impulsive, so free without question. And then the peasants are so splendid. They are such human beings—yes, that is it. Even the man who drives your carriage has—has some real part in what is happening. I remember the evening a party of us, two friends of mine and the wife of one of them, went for a picnic by the Black Sea. We took supper and champagne and ate and drank on the grass. And while we were eating the coachman came up. 'Have a dill pickle,' he said. He wanted to share with us. That seemed to me so right, so—you know what I mean?"

Discuss:

1. What do the details in this passage tell you about the man's attitude toward Russia?

2. What do the details in this passage tell you about the man's attitude toward Vera?

Apply:

Complete the sentence frame below and write a paragraph that supports it with concrete detail.

You'd like almost everything about _____ (a movie, a book, a place, a vacation).

Your selection of detail should allow your reader to understand what you like, why you like it, and how you think it will affect the "you" of the sentence. Share your paragraph with a partner.

Detail

Mansfield: Lesson Two

Consider:

"Before I met you," he said, "I had never spoken of myself to anybody. How well I remember one night, the night that I brought you the little Christmas tree, telling you all about my childhood. And of how I was so miserable that I ran away and lived under a cart in our yard for two days without being discovered. And you listened, and your eyes shone, and I felt that you had even made the little Christmas tree listen too, as in a fairy story."

But of that evening she had remembered a little pot of caviare [caviar]. It had cost seven and sixpence. He could not get over it. Think of it—a tiny jar like that costing seven and sixpence. While she ate it he watched her, delighted and shocked.

"No, really, that is eating money. You could not get seven shillings into a little pot that size. Only think of the profit they must make. . . ." And he had begun some immensely complicated calculations. . . .

Discuss:

1. What does the detail in the first paragraph reveal about the man's character?

2. What do the differences in the details the characters remember about that night reveal about their relationship?

Apply:

Think of an event that you have shared with a friend or family member in the past but remember in totally different ways. Describe the incident from the two perspectives, using specific detail to express the sharply different memories of the event. If you haven't experienced something like that, use your imagination!

Figurative Language
Mansfield: Lesson One

Consider:

As he spoke, so lightly, tapping the end of his cigarette against the ash-tray, she felt the strange beast that had slumbered so long within her bosom stir, stretch itself, yawn, prick up its ears, and suddenly bound to its feet, and fix its longing, hungry stare upon those far away places.

Discuss:

1. Identify the metaphor in the passage above and its literal and figurative terms.

2. How does this metaphor contribute to the reader's understanding of Vera?

Apply:

Think about a time you were exceptionally hungry. Now write an extended metaphor (like Mansfield's) that provides insight into the sensations of extreme hunger. Share your metaphor with the class.

Figurative Language
Mansfield: Lesson Two

Consider:

"What I really wanted then," he said softly, "was to be a sort of carpet—to make myself into a sort of carpet for you to walk on so that you need not be hurt by the sharp stones and the mud that you hated so. It was nothing more positive than that—nothing more selfish. Only I did desire, eventually, to turn into a magic carpet and carry you away to all those lands you longed to see."

Discuss:

1. Identify the metaphor in this passage and its literal and figurative terms.

2. How does this metaphor contribute to the reader's understanding of the man and his relationship to Vera?

Apply:

Write a metaphor that expresses how you would like to treat someone you care about. Extend your metaphor as Mansfield does.

Imagery

Mansfield: Lesson One

Consider:

But she was thinking how well she remembered that trick of his—the trick of interrupting her—and of how it used to exasperate her six years ago. She used to feel then as though he, quite suddenly, in the middle of what she was saying, put his hand over her lips, turned from her, attended to something different, and then took his hand away, and with just the same slightly too broad smile, gave her his attention again. . . . Now we are ready. That is settled.

Discuss:

1. How does the visual and tactile imagery of this passage allow the reader to clearly understand his *trick of interrupting her*?

2. How would the effect of this passage be different if Mansfield had ended it at the end of the first sentence?

Apply:

Work in groups of three. One person should read the passage aloud. The second person should demonstrate the actions of the man. The third person should demonstrate the actions of the woman. Be certain that your facial expressions and actions reflect a careful interpretation of the characters.

Imagery

Mansfield: Lesson Two

Consider:

Do you remember that first afternoon we spent together at Kew Gardens? You were so surprised because I did not know the names of any flowers. I am still just as ignorant for all your telling me. But whenever it is very fine and warm, and I see some bright colours—it's awfully strange—I hear your voice saying: 'Geranium, marigold and verbena.' And I feel those three words are all I recall of some forgotten, heavenly language. . . . You remember that afternoon?"

"Oh, yes, very well." She drew a long, soft breath, as though the paper daffodils between them were almost too sweet to bear. Yet, what had remained in her mind of that particular afternoon was an absurd scene over the tea table. A great many people taking tea in a Chinese pagoda, and he behaving like a maniac about the wasps—waving them away, flapping at them with his straw hat, serious and infuriated out of all proportion to the occasion. How delighted the sniggering tea drinkers had been. And how she had suffered.

Discuss:

1. What kind of imagery does the man use to describe the afternoon at Kew Gardens? What insight does this imagery give the reader about the man's character?

2. Note that Vera remembers that afternoon quite differently. What kind of imagery does she use? What insight does this imagery give the reader about Vera's character?

Apply:

Write two paragraphs using imagery to describe an incident from two vastly different points of view. The first paragraph should use auditory imagery. The second paragraph should use visual imagery. Share your paragraphs with a partner and see if your partner can accurately identify the different points of view, based on the images you used.

Syntax

Mansfield: Lesson One

Consider:

AND then, after six years, she saw him again. He was seated at one of those little bamboo tables decorated with a Japanese vase of paper daffodils. There was a tall plate of fruit in front of him, and very carefully, in a way she recognized immediately as his "special" way, he was peeling an orange.

Discuss:

1. The first sentence in this paragraph is a periodic sentence, a sentence that makes the reader wait until the end of the sentence for the main idea. What effect does this have on the reader?

2. How does the form of the third sentence imitate and reinforce the meaning?

Apply:

Write a periodic sentence about getting a bad grade on a test. Use Mansfield's first sentence as a model. Share your sentence with a partner.

Syntax

Mansfield: Lesson Two

Consider:

"Do you remember that boatman's song that you used to play?"

"Yes." It began to play in her mind as she spoke.

"Do you ever play it now?"

"No, I've no piano."

He was amazed at that. "But what has become of your beautiful piano?"

She made a little grimace. "Sold. Ages ago."

Discuss:

1. What effect does sentence length have on this passage?

2. The passage ends with two sentence fragments. How would the impact of the passage change if it ended like this?

   "It was sold ages ago."

Apply:

Using dialogue, capture a conversation between you and a friend about music. End your dialogue with two short sentence fragments that are abrupt and final. Share your passage with the class and explain how your syntax reinforces meaning. Use Mansfield's passage as a model.

Tone

Mansfield: Lesson Two

Consider:

Think about Mansfield's voice, her tone in this story, and how she uses the elements of voice to develop her theme. Now that you have looked more deeply into the way the story is crafted, answer the discussion questions again to see if your understanding of the author's theme, tone, and voice has changed.

Discuss:

1. What is the tone of the story? Consider the attitude of the characters toward each other and the implied attitude of the author toward the characters. How would you describe the author's voice?

2. What is the theme of this story? How does the tone support the theme of the story?

Apply:

Write a brief analysis of the theme of the story and how the theme is conveyed. Consider the elements of voice and how they contribute to tone and meaning. You should also consider characterization in your analysis. Use textual support as evidence for your analysis.

Your Turn

Mansfield: Culminating Lesson

Consider:

Think about Mansfield's story and how she creates her tone and voice. Now write a story of your own about a chance meeting with someone you used to know. In this story, you will develop your own theme and tone and express your own voice.

Discuss:

1. Think about the theme of your story and how you might develop this theme. Discuss it with a partner.

2. After you write your story, analyze how you express your tone and voice using diction, detail, figurative language, imagery, and syntax.

Apply:

Write a story about a chance meeting with someone you used to know. Approach it any way you like, but be consistent, creative, and clear. Be certain you use all of the elements of voice to shape your tone and express your voice.

Discussion Suggestions

Katherine Mansfield, "A Dill Pickle," *Bliss and Other Stories*

Tone: Lesson One

1. I have split the tone lessons so that students can see how a close analysis of a complex text increases their understanding of both tone and voice. Tone: Lesson Two, repeats the questions of Lesson One to see how students have grown in understanding of the ways authors build tone and express voice. This question helps students think about the connection between attitude and tone and how attitude shapes the author's voice. In discussing this question with students, I suggest that you accept all answers and write them on a chart without judgment. You can then compare their answers after students have experienced the lessons about the other elements of voice.

2. Because this is a short story, we are not interested so much in thesis as we are in theme, the underlying meaning or concern of the work. We are also interested in how the theme of the story aligns with the tone or how tone supports the theme. Again, in this lesson, I suggest that you accept all answers and write them on a chart without judgment. You can then compare answers after students have experienced the lessons about the other elements of voice.

Diction: Lesson One

1. Her *high fur collar* that she must *unbutton* is partly the style of the time. More importantly, though, it indicates a character that is closed, buttoned up, secure and safe, unable to open up to either love or adventure. Although she dreams of adventure, she seems unable to actually experience it. In fact, she doesn't feel well once her *high fur collar* is *unbuttoned.*

2. The changed lines have a totally different connotation. She *loosens* her collar, a more casual and relaxed gesture. And the collar is made of lace, a more open and decorative fabric. With these lines, we no longer see Vera as uptight, straight-laced, and closed in her own world.

Diction: Lesson Two

1. A *half laugh* is an ironic laugh at something that is not particularly funny. Here it is an acknowledgment that the man recognizes the irony of his travels: that the travel plans they made together he fulfilled alone. The man acknowledges their past plans but also accepts the fact that he has gone to most of the places they had planned to go together. He seems to accept the way life has turned out as his due.

2. Substituting *poetic justice* for *curious* adds a bitter edge to his observation. In the original he finds it strange, but it's not payback. He isn't attacking her for the breakup letter she wrote so long before. The changed diction makes the passage more acrimonious and vengeful than the original.

Detail: Lesson One

1. The details in the passage underscore a positive, almost idolizing, attitude toward Russia. He praises *almost everything about Russian life*. It is *informal, impulsive, free*. The peasants are *splendid*. He then recounts the incident of the coachman sharing a dill pickle at the picnic. This gesture comes to represent freedom, adventure, and companionship, qualities both characters seem to lack at the time of the encounter.

2. The man expects Vera to understand his fascination with Russian life. This is partly based on what he remembers about her from six years prior, when they were planning adventures together. He assumes she would *like almost everything about Russian life*. And he asks for her confirmation of the significance of the dill pickle: *That seemed to me so right, so—you know what I mean?* However, his attitude is complex. He wants her to understand, assumes she will understand; yet he does not acknowledge the fact that she can only know what the experience was like vicariously. He is absorbed in his own feelings and experiences and fairly insensitive to hers.

Detail: Lesson Two

1. The detail of the first paragraph reveals a self-centered romantic. He remembers the *little Christmas tree* and how she listens to his stories of a sad childhood. He carries this further into the *fairy* world of listening trees. His memories are centered on himself. She is there to listen. The memory he recreates is one of magic, brought to light through her attention. He focuses on the magic and pleasure (for him) of their relationship.

2. Her memories of that night are altogether different. She remembers only conflict over the cost of the caviar. She is pragmatic and negative, focused on the conflicts of their relationship. It will be interesting to see students' perspectives about the characters' past relationship. Some find him totally self-absorbed and insensitive. Some find her cold and judgmental. Perhaps both of these views are correct. Or perhaps their relationship was altogether different—the potential for communication and understanding thwarted by circumstance. There is much room for discussion here.

Figurative Language: Lesson One

1. The metaphor is the comparison of her desires to the *strange beast* inside her. The literal term is implied: her desire for adventure, for visiting *far away places*. The figurative term is *the strange beast that had slumbered so long*. In other words, the conversation awakens her long-dormant desire for travel and adventure in the same way as an animal awakens from sleep, stretches, yawns, jumps up, and stares at what it wants.

2. The metaphor helps the reader understand just how repressed Vera is. The beast that had *slumbered so long* awakens slowly and stares longingly and hungrily at what it cannot have. Like the beast, Vera slowly recognizes her desires but only stares hungrily at the *far away places* she will never visit.

Figurative Language: Lesson Two

1. The metaphor in this passage compares the man to a carpet that protects Vera and then a magic carpet that takes her to the lands she longs to see. The literal term is the man and the figurative term is a carpet for protection and a magic carpet for adventure.

2. The metaphor underscores the man's romantic nature, wanting to take care of Vera and whisk her away. But it also reveals his complete lack of understanding of her nature. She is pragmatic and realistic, not likely to run away on a magic carpet even if she wants to. She doesn't want to be taken care of. Their relationship is at cross-purposes and devoid of real understanding. That's the way I see it. It will be interesting to see how the students understand this relationship.

Imagery: Lesson One

1. The imagery brings the reader into the scene, making the interruption concrete and easily pictured. It also makes the interruption physical, visceral, and allows the reader to feel the interruption as well as see it.

2. The reader could understand Vera's attitude and irritation without the visual and tactile images that follow, but the passage would lose its immediacy. The imagery transforms the *trick* from an abstract statement of an irritating interruption to a vivid and immediate action that allows the reader to fully understand the source of the irritation for Vera.

Imagery: Lesson Two

1. The man uses visual, tactile, and auditory images to describe the afternoon at Kew Gardens. And all of his imagery is veiled in a romantic haze. He thinks of that afternoon whenever it is very fine and warm (tactile) or when he sees bright colours (visual). Most importantly, he hears her voice naming the flowers, and he thinks of that voice as some *forgotten, heavenly language* (auditory). What he remembers is beautiful, almost unworldly. The imagery reveals his nature as romantic, wistful, and focused only on good memories, especially as they pertain to him.

2. Vera remembers that afternoon quite differently. She uses sight imagery to describe a scene that she finds embarrassing and *absurd*. She sees many people having tea and pictures his behavior about the wasps. He is *behaving like a maniac . . . waving them away, flapping at them with his straw hat, serious and infuriated out of all proportion to the occasion*. Gone are the romantic sounds and fine weather. The imagery shows Vera to be cold and judgmental, remembering the afternoon only as it reflects on her. Perhaps he is right when he says later, *". . . we were [and still are] such egoists, so self-engrossed, so wrapped up in ourselves that we hadn't a corner in our hearts for anybody else."* Of course, there are other ways to view these two characters. It will be interesting to see how the students view them.

Syntax: Lesson One

1. A periodic sentence creates syntactic tension and emphasizes the ideas that are presented at the end of the sentence. This sentence starts with a conjunction; in fact, the story itself starts with a conjunction. Starting with *and* gives the reader a feeling that this is not a new story but a continuation of an old one. So it is. She sees him again *after six years*, and the story begins. Seeing him again, remembering the past and noting what has changed and what has not, leads the reader into the story's central themes and conflict.

2. The focus on the third sentence is also on the last part of the sentence, his *peeling an orange*. But the syntax of this sentence not only keeps the reader waiting for resolution but also helps the reader understand *his "special" way"* of peeling an orange. The sentence unravels in the same way that the man peels an orange. It starts with an independent clause (*There was a tall plate of fruit in front of him*). This simple observation is followed by a series of phrases and clauses that slows the reader down, like the careful peeling of an orange. The form of the sentence helps the reader "see" the incident as Vera sees it.

Syntax: Lesson Two

1. Although all of the sentences are relatively short, it is interesting to note that the longer sentences are his words and her thoughts. His words are surface questions, circling around but self-absorbed and unable to connect to Vera's life. Her responses to his questions are short and abrupt. The brevity of her replies is in contrast to her thoughts, emphasizing her closed nature and inability to connect to the man. Sentence length thus helps the reader understand the characters and the themes of this story.

2. Using a complete sentence rather than the two sentence fragments weakens the effect of the passage. It is just a simple sentence that neither discourages further discussion nor encourages it. The fragments, however, are curt, final, and abrupt. They allow no further conversation; indeed, they cut off all discussion. The syntax thus reinforces what the reader is learning about Vera: that she is cold, closed, and unable to connect.

Tone: Lesson Two

1. This lesson repeats the questions of Tone: Lesson One to see how students have grown in their understanding of the ways authors build tone and express voice. This question helps students think about the connection between attitude and tone and how attitude shapes the author's voice. The tone of this story can be described as critical (of the characters), cynical, or disparaging of relationships in general. The man remembers Vera only by the way she listens to him. Vera remembers the man largely through the uncomfortable encounters they have had. Yet there is still something, a kind of yearning, between them, which is, of course, unsatisfied. The reader is left with a feeling that the only reality is loneliness and isolation. As students discuss these questions again, take notes on a large chart. Compare this chart with the chart you developed with students at the beginning of this section. Lead a discussion about the ways close analysis of a piece of writing deepens with knowledge of the elements of voice.

2. Because this is a short story, we are not interested so much in thesis as we are in theme, the underlying meaning or concern of the work. The themes here are the inability to connect, self-absorption, lost love, lack of communication. We are also interested in how the themes of the story align with the tone or how tone supports the themes. In this story, the tone, created through selection of diction, detail, figurative language, imagery, and syntax, supports the themes of alienation, lost love, and failure to communicate. Students may express different answers to these questions. Their answers are acceptable, of course, if they can support their answers with evidence from the text. As in Question 1, take notes on a chart while students discuss these questions. Compare this chart with the one you developed with students at the beginning of this section. Lead a discussion about the ways close analysis of a piece of writing deepens with knowledge of the elements of voice.

Your Turn: Culminating Lesson

1. If students have trouble deciding on a focus or theme, it would be helpful to take some time to guide them in ways (modeling, brainstorming, graphic organizers, freewriting) to find a topic, narrow their approach, and gather ideas. It would also be helpful to give students quiet time to think and then time to discuss ideas in pairs or small groups. Ultimately, students will have to decide on their own themes and how they will develop them; but support and guidance never hurt. What they decide will determine their tone and help shape their voice. Students should jot down their themes and some ideas about development to keep in mind as they draft their essays.

2. This question is better addressed after students write their first draft. Students can then analyze the tone and voice they have captured in their stories and the tools they used to develop tone and voice. By now they should understand that they have the power to craft a specific tone through focused use of the elements of voice. If they keep a specific tone in mind, they will shape their stories in such a way as to reveal their tone to their readers. Voice is individual and distinctive. Is their voice clear? Is it exuberant? Detached? Critical? Affirming? For this assignment, students should have the freedom to shape their own voices through the skillful use of the elements of voice.

Sir Francis Bacon,
"Of Studies," *The Essays or Counsels, Civil and Moral*

STUDIES serve for delight, for ornament, and for ability. Their chief use for delight, is in privateness and retiring; for ornament, is in discourse; and for ability, is in the judgment, and disposition of business. For expert men can execute, and perhaps judge of particulars, one by one; but the general counsels, and the plots and marshalling of affairs, come best, from those that are learned. To spend too much time in studies is sloth; to use them too much for ornament, is affectation; to make judgment wholly by their rules, is the humor of a scholar. They perfect nature, and are perfected by experience: for natural abilities are like natural plants, that need proyning, by study; and studies themselves, do give forth directions too much at large, except they be bounded in by experience. Crafty men contemn studies, simple men admire them, and wise men use them; for they teach not their own use; but that is a wisdom without them, and above them, won by observation. Read not to contradict and confute; nor to believe and take for granted; nor to find talk and discourse; but to weigh and consider. Some books are to be tasted, others to be swallowed, and some few to be chewed and digested; that is, some books are to be read only in parts; others to be read, but not curiously; and some few to be read wholly, and with diligence and attention. Some books also may be read by deputy, and extracts made of them by others; but that would be only in the less important arguments, and the meaner sort of books, else distilled books are like common distilled waters, flashy things. Reading maketh a full man; conference a ready man; and writing an exact man. And therefore, if a man write little, he had need have a great memory; if he confer little, he had need have a present wit: and if he read little, he had need have much cunning, to seem to know, that he doth not. Histories make men wise; poets witty; the mathematics subtile; natural philosophy deep; moral grave; logic and rhetoric able to contend. Abeunt studia in mores. Nay, there is no stond or impediment in the wit, but may be wrought out by fit studies; like as diseases of the body, may have appropriate exercises. Bowling is good for the stone and reins; shooting for the lungs and breast; gentle walking for the stomach; riding for the head; and the like. So if a man's wit be wandering, let him study the mathematics; for in demonstrations, if his wit be called away never so little, he must begin again. If his wit be not apt to distinguish or find differences, let him study the Schoolmen; for they are cymini sectores. If he be not apt to beat over matters, and to call up one thing to prove and illustrate another, let him study the lawyers' cases. So every defect of the mind, may have a special receipt.

To the Student:

♣ Sir Francis Bacon was an English writer and scientist who lived in the 16th and early 17th centuries. He is often considered the father of the scientific method. Because he wrote so long ago, you may have some problems with the language. There are differences in spelling (*proyning* for *pruning*; *maketh* for *makes*; *subtile* for *subtle*). Bacon also uses several Latin phrases (*abeunt studia in mores*: studies become habits; *cymini secores*: hair splitters). And he uses the word *man* to mean all people, as was the convention of the time. This essay is short; however, you will need to read it slowly and multiple times in order to fully understand it. The style and voice is probably quite different from what you are used to. This is a formal essay, an author's opinion or argument that is serious and coherent, well supported but short. The topic is not particularly controversial (although it might have been somewhat more controversial in its time), but it is thought-provoking. And the argument is presented in a very methodical and logical fashion. The pleasure here comes from observing Bacon's verbal self-confidence, noting the precision of support, and analyzing the careful balance in his prose style and thought. In Bacon's worldview, study and careful thinking are essential. In this essay, he is delineating the justification of his beliefs.

Tone

Bacon: Lesson One

Consider:

Read the essay several times slowly and carefully. Use underlining or highlighting and marginal notes to help you clarify parts of the essay you do not understand. Look up any words you do not know.

Discuss:

1. Identify the purpose and thesis of this essay. Who is the audience?

2. What is the tone of the essay? How would you describe the author's voice?

Apply:

Write two paragraphs about homework. In the first paragraph your audience is your local school board. In the second paragraph your audience is your peers. Share your paragraphs with one or two other students.

Bacon: Lesson One

Consider:

Crafty men contemn studies, simple men admire them, and wise men use them; for they teach not their own use; but that is a wisdom without them, and above them, won by observation.

Discuss:

1. Look up the word *crafty*. Does the word have a positive or negative connotation in this essay? How do you know?

2. How does the use of this word help you understand the tone of the passage?

Apply:

Write two original sentences that contain the word *simple*. In the first sentence, give the word a positive connotation; in the second sentence, give the word a negative connotation. Share your sentences with another student.

Bacon: Lesson Two

Consider:

So if a man's wit be **wandering**, let him study the mathematics;

Discuss:

1. Why do you think Bacon uses the word *wandering* to describe wit (intelligence, understanding) that is improved by studying mathematics?

2. How would it change the meaning of the reference if Bacon had written *So if a man's wit be weak, let him study mathematics*?

Apply:

Write a sentence about improving memory. Think about words that are clear, concrete, and exact, like Bacon's. Use the sentence frame below, or create a sentence of your own.

If a person's memory is _____, he or she should _____

_____

_____ .

Bacon: Lesson One

Consider:

Read not to contradict and confute; nor to believe and take for granted; nor to find talk and discourse; but to weigh and consider.

Discuss:

1. Here Bacon does not use detail to describe a scene or situation. What kind of detail does Bacon use here?

2. How does the use of detail help the reader understand Bacon's attitude toward studies?

Apply:

Write a paragraph to support this statement: *Reading is excellent exercise for the brain.* In your paragraph use at least three details that support the statement and ensure that your reader agrees with the assertion.

Detail

Bacon: Lesson Two

Consider:

STUDIES serve for delight, for ornament, and for ability. Their chief use for delight, is in privateness and retiring; for ornament, is in discourse; and for ability, is in the judgment, and disposition of business.

Discuss:

1. Bacon supports the abstract contention of his first sentence (*STUDIES serve for delight, for ornament, and for ability*) with detail in the second sentence. How does the detail of the second sentence make the abstraction of the first sentence more concrete and understandable?

2. How does Bacon's use of detail contribute to your understanding of the writer's voice?

Apply:

Write two sentences explaining the benefits of exercise. Your first sentence should state the benefits in general terms, and your second sentence should use detail to make the benefits more concrete and specific.

Figurative Language

Bacon: Lesson One

Consider:

Some books are to be tasted, others to be swallowed, and some few to be chewed and digested; that is, some books are to be read only in parts; others to be read, but not curiously; and some few to be read wholly, and with diligence and attention.

Discuss:

1. The metaphor in this passage has three parts. What are the three parts of the metaphor, and what are their literal and figurative terms?

2. How does the use of metaphor enrich the meaning of the passage?

Apply:

Think of a metaphor for a party. Now think of three levels of enjoyment of a party that can be expressed by a modification of this metaphor. Using Bacon's food metaphor as a model, write a sentence expressing all three parts of this metaphor.

Figurative Language

Bacon: Lesson Two

Consider:

Nay, there is no stond [hindrance] or impediment in the wit, but may be wrought out by fit studies; like as diseases of the body, may have appropriate exercises.

Discuss:

1. What is the simile in this sentence? What are the literal and figurative terms?

2. What does this simile reveal about Bacon's attitude toward studies?

Apply:

Write a sentence using a simile to compare a good meal (the literal term) to something not usually considered to be similar. Share your sentence with another student and discuss what the simile adds to the reader's understanding of a good meal.

Bacon: Lesson One

Consider:

Some books are to be tasted, others to be swallowed, and some few to be chewed and digested;

Discuss:

1. Although this passage is a metaphor, it is also a gustatory image. How does the use of an image help shape your understanding of the different kinds of books?

2. How would it change the power of this passage if Bacon had written it like this?

    Some books should be skimmed, some read without thinking,
    and some read slowly and deeply;

Apply:

Think of three different kinds of movies and an auditory or visual image you could use to categorize them. Now write a sentence using the image to classify the kinds of movies. Base your sentence on Bacon's sentence above. Your image can be figurative or not.

Bacon: Lesson Two

Consider:

> . . . natural abilities are like natural plants, that need proyning [pruning],
> by study;

Discuss:

1. This passage is figurative, here a simile. But it is also a visual image. What does the image help you see?

2. How does the visual image help the reader understand the importance of study?

Apply:

Write a sentence or phrase that uses an image to capture the importance of practice in sports. Be certain that your image sharply evokes a sight, sound, touch, taste, or smell. Your image can be figurative or not. Share your image with another student and discuss its impact on the reader.

Syntax

Bacon: Lesson One

Consider:

Studies serve for delight, for ornament, and for ability. Their chief use for delight, is in privateness and retiring; for ornament, is in discourse; and for ability, is in the judgment, and disposition of business.

Discuss:

1. Bacon starts the essay with a short sentence. What is the purpose of this sentence, and how does sentence length contribute to the sentence's purpose?

2. What is the purpose of the second, longer sentence? What does the sentence structure in this passage reveal about the author's voice?

Apply:

Write a long sentence to extend and develop the short sentence below. Use Bacon's sentence as a model.

Music serves for pleasure, bonding, and contemplation.

Syntax

Bacon: Lesson Two

Consider:

Reading maketh a full man; conference a ready man; and writing an exact man. And therefore, if a man write little, he had need have a great memory; if he confer little, he had need have a present wit: and if he read little, he had need have much cunning, to seem to know, that he doth not.

Discuss:

1. Examine the first sentence in the passage above. Remember that semicolons are used to separate and give equal weight to independent clauses. Here the verbs in the second and third independent clauses (*maketh*) are understood, but they are still there. How does the structure of this sentence reveal the author's voice?

2. Note that each clause in the second sentence is an *if . . . then* statement, creating then resolving syntactic tension. Notice also that Bacon reverses the order of reading and writing in his clauses. Both of these techniques shift sentence weight toward the end of the sentence. How does this shift in sentence weight affect the reader's understanding of the sentence's meaning? How does this sentence structure help establish the tone of the essay?

Apply:

Write a sentence with three independent clauses separated by semicolons. Your verbs in the second and third clauses may be stated or understood. You may choose your own topic or write about music or video games. Try to write a balanced and orderly sentence with a serious and confident tone.

Tone

Bacon: Lesson Two

Consider:

Think about Bacon's voice, his tone in this essay, and how he uses the elements of voice to accomplish his purpose. Now that you have looked more deeply into the way the essay is crafted, answer the discussion questions again to see if your understanding of Bacon's purpose, thesis, tone, and voice has changed.

Discuss:

1. Identify the purpose, audience, and thesis of the essay.

2. What is the tone of the essay? How would you describe the author's voice?

Apply:

Write a brief essay analyzing the meaning and purpose of Bacon's essay and how meaning is conveyed. Consider the elements of voice and how they contribute to both purpose and **meaning. Use textual support as evidence for your analysis.**

Your Turn

Bacon: Culminating Lesson

Consider:

Think about Bacon's essay and how he creates his tone and voice. Now write an essay of your own on the topic of studies. In this essay, you will develop your own tone and express your own voice.

Discuss:

1. Identify the purpose and thesis of your essay. Who is your audience?

2. How will you express your tone and voice using diction, detail, figurative language, imagery, and syntax?

Apply:

Write an essay on studies. Approach it any way you like, but be consistent and clear. Be certain you use the elements of voice to shape your tone and express your voice.

Discussion Suggestions

Sir Francis Bacon, "Of Studies," *The Essays or Counsels, Civil and Moral*

Tone: Lesson One

1. I have split the tone lessons so that students can see how a close analysis of a difficult text increases their understanding of both tone and voice. Tone: Lesson Two repeats the questions of Lesson One to see how students have grown in understanding of the ways authors build tone and express voice. This question stresses the importance of purpose, audience, and thesis, or main idea, as determiners of tone and voice. In discussing this question with students, I suggest that you accept all answers and write them on a chart without judgment. You can then compare their answers after students have experienced the lessons about the other elements of voice.

2. Here it is important that students understand the difference between tone and voice. Tone is the author's attitude toward his or her subject or audience. Voice is the personality of the author, as revealed through his or her use of the elements of voice. They are often closely related but not always. Again, in this lesson, I suggest that you accept all answers and write them on a chart without judgment. You can then compare answers after students have experienced the lessons about the other elements of voice.

Diction: Lesson One

1. Here the word *crafty* has a negative connotation, meaning cunning or deceitful. Partly it is the most common definition, but it is also associated with men who *contemn studies*. This essay establishes a case for the importance of studies; people who treat studies with contempt are viewed in a negative light.

2. The tone of the passage is confident, didactic, and assured. Bacon is not suggesting he is right; he is certain. Using the word *crafty* to describe *men who contemn studies* underscores his confident tone. Those who disdain studies, which he forcefully advocates, are condemned as deceitful, underhanded, and sly.

Diction: Lesson Two

1. The word *wandering* connotes a kind of purposelessness. People wander when they have no plan or fixed purpose. Mathematics is orderly and logical. It is the perfect antidote for training a wandering mind.

2. The word *weak* is imprecise and abstract. Just what is weak about the man's mind? The sentence loses its precision and specificity. The remedy—training through studying mathematics—is no longer clearly applicable.

Detail: Lesson One

1. The detail here takes the form of reasons. Bacon supports the idea that the best purpose for reading is contemplation. He supports his contention with reasons <u>not</u> to read: to argue, to become complacent, or to have something to talk about.

2. The use of detail clarifies Bacon's attitude toward studies, that studies have a clear purpose and must be used wisely. Detail makes abstract thought more specific and concrete.

Detail: Lesson Two

1. The detail in the second sentence provides examples of what Bacon means when he writes of *delight, ornament,* and *ability.* The detail here helps the reader understand the purpose of studies and clarifies the abstractions of the first sentence.

2. The detail is assured, balanced, and logical, like the rest of Bacon's essay. To illustrate the purposes of studies, Bacon chooses privacy and rest, conversation, and good judgment. He presents his choice of details as if there could be no other purpose for studies, and he does so in a sentence that is orderly, balanced, and clear. His use of detail reinforces his rational, logical, and self-confident voice.

Figurative Language: Lesson One

1. We also study this part of the passage in Imagery: Lesson One. The reference to books being tasted, swallowed, and chewed and digested is both a gustatory image and a metaphor. The three parts of the metaphor and their literal and figurative terms are as follows:

   a. Some books should be read [like] food that is merely tasted. The literal term is *some books*, and the figurative term is food that is merely tasted.

   b. Other books should be read [like] food that is swallowed but not really tasted. The literal term is *other books*, and the figurative term is food that is swallowed but not really tasted.

   c. Some few books should be read [like] food that is chewed and digested. The literal term is *some few books*, and the figurative term is food that is chewed and digested.

2. The metaphor connects something that may be new to the reader (that not all books should be treated equally) with something familiar (that not all foods are equally delicious and nutritious). This is, of course, one of the purposes of metaphor—to shed light on the unfamiliar by comparing it with the familiar. It strengthens Bacon's argument about the importance of study in developing judgment, and it does that by giving readers a metaphor they can fully understand.

Figurative Language: Lesson Two

1. The simile is a little complicated because of the diction and syntax, but students should be able to sort it out if they take their time. The simile may be stated something like this: Incorrect thinking can be improved by appropriate studies just as poor health can be improved by appropriate exercise. The literal term is incorrect thinking improved by appropriate study. The figurative term is poor health improved by appropriate exercise.

2. The simile reveals a sure but guarded attitude toward study. Bacon never says that studies are the solution to every problem. He advocates study, of course, but tempers it by the word *fit*. The study must be appropriate to the defects in thought. He carries this belief through the figurative term of the simile. Diseases may be corrected by exercise, but it must be the right type of exercise.

Imagery: Lesson One

1. We also study this part of the passage in Figurative Language: Lesson One. The image, which is also a metaphor, makes Bacon's distinctions among books clear and vivid. It brings the reader into the conversation, with his reference to differences among foods, something we are all familiar with.

2. The sentence loses its power without the gustatory images. Although the new sentence is clear, it just sounds didactic, even bossy. The gustatory images bring the reader into the experience and make the distinctions lively—clearly related to common understandings. Bacon retains his logical and confident tone, but he helps the reader to appreciate the different values of books by evoking a common experience through imagery.

Imagery: Lesson Two

1. The visual image evokes a scene of wild plants in need of trimming and pruning. The plants may be beautiful, but they lack discipline and order. In Bacon's world view, the plants *need* pruning, implying that the wild plants would be improved by making them look more orderly, disciplined, and trim.

2. The image gives insight to another use of study: disciplining and thereby improving natural intellectual gifts.

Syntax: Lesson One

1. The purpose of the short sentence is to state the thesis of the essay. In English, crucial ideas are generally stated in short sentences; longer sentences extend, explain, or illustrate the contention of the short sentence. Bacon's purpose is to convince readers of the importance of appropriate study. This sentence clearly and concisely reveals his purpose and draws attention to that purpose through the directness and brevity of the sentence.

2. The second longer sentence explains and extends the short first sentence. The second sentence refers back to the first sentence and extends by example and detail, thus clarifying and illustrating his meaning. The structure of these sentences reveals an author who is orderly, well-reasoned, and sure. Each sentence is divided into three parts, for balance and proportion, with each part of the second sentence reflecting and extending the corresponding part of the first sentence. Bacon never considers an opposing view or leaves room for doubt. (He never says *There are many purposes for study, but I think. . . .*) His trust in the absolute truth of his beliefs reveals the voice of a self-confident and rational thinker.

Syntax: Lesson Two

1. The chief characteristics of Bacon's voice are his self-confidence and his balanced way of thinking. Bacon uses three independent clauses that are in perfect balance in terms of structure (subject/verb/complement). He uses a short sentence to introduce the idea, emphasizing the strength of his conviction. And he uses active verbs to emphasize the power of reading, conversation, and writing. This sentence exemplifies Bacon's voice: sure (he never considers the possibility that others may have differing opinions); composed (there is careful order in his thinking and expression); and strong (his statements are direct and clear).

2. Shifting the weight to the end of a sentence makes the reader wait for the meaning of the sentence. It helps keep the reader focused, adding tension that needs to be resolved. Thus, the reader wants to know what will happen *if a man [sic] write little . . . confer little . . . read little.* Bacon, of course, resolves the tension: If one doesn't write much, he or she better have a good memory; if one doesn't discuss much, he or she better have quick intelligence that needs little practice; if one reads little, he or she better be sly and skilled in pretending to know things he or she does not know. The reversal of the order of reading and writing in the second sentence also throws the emphasis of the sentence toward the end of the sentence, toward reading, the foundation of studies. Notice also that the final clause is longer than the other clauses and is preceded by a colon, punctuation that directs the reader's attention to the important words that follow. Reading is central, Bacon says with his syntax. All studies are grounded in reading. This sentence—indeed, all of Bacon's sentences—helps establish the rational, careful, and confident tone of the essay. Sentences are balanced, orderly, and studied in their construction. This reflects the rational, methodical, and confident tone of the essay.

Tone: Lesson Two

1. I have split the tone lessons so that students can see how a close analysis of a difficult text increases their understanding of both tone and voice. This lesson repeats the questions of Tone: Lesson One to see how students have grown in understanding of the ways authors build tone and express voice; and the question stresses the importance of purpose, audience, and thesis as determiners of tone and voice. Possible purposes for this essay include to instruct, to inform, to convince readers of the importance of appropriate study, to explore the nature of appropriate study, and the like. The thesis is stated in the first sentence: *STUDIES serve for delight, for ornament, and for ability.* The rest of the essay supports this thesis. The audience, as we can infer from the diction, syntax, and tone, is primarily Bacon's educated peers. Any variation of these answers is acceptable as long as students support their answers with evidence from the text. As students discuss these questions again, take notes on a large chart. Compare this chart with the chart you developed with students at the beginning of this section. Lead a discussion about the ways close analysis of a piece of writing deepens with knowledge of the elements of voice.

2. Review the difference between tone and voice with your students. Tone is the author's attitude toward his or her subject or audience. Voice is the personality of the author, as revealed through his or her use of the elements of voice. Here the tone and voice are virtually the same, but that is not always true. Students may express different answers to these questions. Their answers are acceptable, of course, if they can support their answers with evidence from the text. Bacon's tone in this essay is respectful (he expects his readers to understand him), didactic (he is teaching the "right" approach to studies), and self-assured (students may even say arrogant, which they could certainly make a case for). His voice is confident, logical, orderly, and balanced (again, students may say something like egotistical, which is fine as long as they support their answers with evidence from the text). As in Question 1, take notes on a chart while students discuss these questions. Compare this chart with the one you developed with students at the beginning of this section. Lead a discussion about the ways close analysis of a piece of writing deepens with knowledge of the elements of voice.

Your Turn: Culminating Lesson

1. If students have trouble deciding on a specific topic or thesis, it would be helpful to take some time to guide them in ways (modeling, brainstorming, graphic organizers, freewriting) to find a workable topic, narrow their approach, and gather ideas. It would also be helpful to give students quiet time to think and then time to discuss ideas in pairs or small groups. Ultimately, students will have to decide on their own thesis and how they will develop it; but support and guidance never hurt. What they decide will determine their tone and help shape their voice. Students should write down their purpose, thesis, and audience to keep in mind as they draft their essays.

2. Students will also have to decide the tone they want to develop in their essays. By now they should understand that they have the power to craft a specific tone through focused use of the elements of voice. If they keep a specific tone in mind, they will shape their essays in such a way as to reveal their tone to their readers. Voice is individual and distinctive. Will their essays be passionate? Cool and studied? Ironic? Balanced and rational? Positive? Negative? For this assignment, students should have the freedom to develop their own voices through the skillful use of the elements of voice.

Robert Frost,
"The Death of the Hired Man," *North of Boston*

Mary sat musing on the lamp-flame at the table
Waiting for Warren. When she heard his step,
She ran on tip-toe down the darkened passage
To meet him in the doorway with the news
And put him on his guard. "Silas is back."
She pushed him outward with her through the door
And shut it after her. "Be kind," she said.
She took the market things from Warren's arms
And set them on the porch, then drew him down
To sit beside her on the wooden steps.

"When was I ever anything but kind to him?
But I'll not have the fellow back," he said.
"I told him so last haying, didn't I?
'If he left then,' I said, 'that ended it.'
What good is he? Who else will harbour him
At his age for the little he can do?
What help he is there's no depending on.
Off he goes always when I need him most.
'He thinks he ought to earn a little pay,
Enough at least to buy tobacco with,
So he won't have to beg and be beholden.'
'All right,' I say, 'I can't afford to pay
Any fixed wages, though I wish I could.'
'Someone else can.' 'Then someone else will have to.'
I shouldn't mind his bettering himself
If that was what it was. You can be certain,
When he begins like that, there's someone at him
Trying to coax him off with pocket-money,—
In haying time, when any help is scarce.
In winter he comes back to us. I'm done."

"Sh! not so loud: he'll hear you," Mary said.

"I want him to: he'll have to soon or late."

"He's worn out. He's asleep beside the stove.
When I came up from Rowe's I found him here,
Huddled against the barn-door fast asleep,
A miserable sight, and frightening, too—

You needn't smile—I didn't recognise him—
I wasn't looking for him—and he's changed.
Wait till you see."

                "Where did you say he'd been?"

"He didn't say. I dragged him to the house,
And gave him tea and tried to make him smoke.
I tried to make him talk about his travels.
Nothing would do: he just kept nodding off."

"What did he say? Did he say anything?"

"But little."

                    "Anything? Mary, confess
He said he'd come to ditch the meadow for me."

"Warren!"

                "But did he? I just want to know."

"Of course he did. What would you have him say?
Surely you wouldn't grudge the poor old man
Some humble way to save his self-respect.
He added, if you really care to know,
He meant to clear the upper pasture, too.
That sounds like something you have heard before?
Warren, I wish you could have heard the way
He jumbled everything. I stopped to look
Two or three times—he made me feel so queer—
To see if he was talking in his sleep.
He ran on Harold Wilson—you remember—
The boy you had in haying four years since.
He's finished school, and teaching in his college.
Silas declares you'll have to get him back.
He says they two will make a team for work:
Between them they will lay this farm as smooth!
The way he mixed that in with other things.
He thinks young Wilson a likely lad, though daft
On education—you know how they fought
All through July under the blazing sun,
Silas up on the cart to build the load,
Harold along beside to pitch it on."

"Yes, I took care to keep well out of earshot."

"Well, those days trouble Silas like a dream.
You wouldn't think they would. How some things linger!
Harold's young college boy's assurance piqued him.
After so many years he still keeps finding
Good arguments he sees he might have used.
I sympathise. I know just how it feels
To think of the right thing to say too late.
Harold's associated in his mind with Latin.
He asked me what I thought of Harold's saying
He studied Latin like the violin
Because he liked it—that an argument!
He said he couldn't make the boy believe
He could find water with a hazel prong—
Which showed how much good school had ever done him.
He wanted to go over that. But most of all
He thinks if he could have another chance
To teach him how to build a load of hay———"

"I know, that's Silas' one accomplishment.
He bundles every forkful in its place,
And tags and numbers it for future reference,
So he can find and easily dislodge it
In the unloading. Silas does that well.
He takes it out in bunches like big birds' nests.
You never see him standing on the hay
He's trying to lift, straining to lift himself."

"He thinks if he could teach him that, he'd be
Some good perhaps to someone in the world.
He hates to see a boy the fool of books.
Poor Silas, so concerned for other folk,
And nothing to look backward to with pride,
And nothing to look forward to with hope,
So now and never any different."

Part of a moon was falling down the west,
Dragging the whole sky with it to the hills.
Its light poured softly in her lap. She saw
And spread her apron to it. She put out her hand
Among the harp-like morning-glory strings,
Taut with the dew from garden bed to eaves,

As if she played unheard the tenderness
That wrought on him beside her in the night.
"Warren," she said, "he has come home to die:
You needn't be afraid he'll leave you this time."

"Home," he mocked gently.

                 "Yes, what else but home?
It all depends on what you mean by home.
Of course he's nothing to us, any more
Than was the hound that came a stranger to us
Out of the woods, worn out upon the trail."

"Home is the place where, when you have to go there,
They have to take you in."

                  "I should have called it
Something you somehow haven't to deserve."

Warren leaned out and took a step or two,
Picked up a little stick, and brought it back
And broke it in his hand and tossed it by.
"Silas has better claim on us you think
Than on his brother? Thirteen little miles
As the road winds would bring him to his door.
Silas has walked that far no doubt to-day.
Why didn't he go there? His brother's rich,
A somebody—director in the bank."

"He never told us that."

                  "We know it though."

"I think his brother ought to help, of course.
I'll see to that if there is need. He ought of right
To take him in, and might be willing to—
He may be better than appearances.
But have some pity on Silas. Do you think
If he'd had any pride in claiming kin
Or anything he looked for from his brother,
He'd keep so still about him all this time?"

"I wonder what's between them."

                            "I can tell you.
Silas is what he is—we wouldn't mind him—
But just the kind that kinsfolk can't abide.
He never did a thing so very bad.
He don't know why he isn't quite as good
As anyone. He won't be made ashamed
To please his brother, worthless though he is."

"*I* can't think Si ever hurt anyone."

"No, but he hurt my heart the way he lay
And rolled his old head on that sharp-edged chair-back.
He wouldn't let me put him on the lounge.
You must go in and see what you can do.
I made the bed up for him there to-night.
You'll be surprised at him—how much he's broken.
His working days are done; I'm sure of it."

"I'd not be in a hurry to say that."

"I haven't been. Go, look, see for yourself.
But, Warren, please remember how it is:
He's come to help you ditch the meadow.
He has a plan. You mustn't laugh at him.
He may not speak of it, and then he may.
I'll sit and see if that small sailing cloud
Will hit or miss the moon."

                            It hit the moon.
Then there were three there, making a dim row,
The moon, the little silver cloud, and she.

Warren returned—too soon, it seemed to her,
Slipped to her side, caught up her hand and waited.

"Warren," she questioned.

                         "Dead," was all he answered.

To the Student:

♣ This elegant, narrative poem by Robert Frost, a Pulitzer Prize-winning poet of the 20th century, tells a story; but it is also a contemplation of family, home, acceptance, self-respect, and compassion. Our discussion of this poem will focus on the elements of voice, but there are many other aspects of the poem you may want to explore. The poem is written in blank verse, unrhymed lines of iambic pentameter, a form of poetry also favored by both John Milton and William Shakespeare. You might want to explore the effect blank verse has on the tone of the poem. In addition, you might want to explore the sound devices Frost uses in the poem (alliteration, assonance, consonance, dissonance, and euphony, for example) and the narrative aspects of the poem (characterization, conflict, plot structure, dialogue, and setting). It will take several readings to fully appreciate and understand this complex and thought-provoking poem.

Tone

Frost: Lesson One

Consider:

Read the poem several times slowly and carefully. As with most poems, it's best to read the poem aloud—with a partner or in a small group. Use underlining or highlighting and marginal notes to indicate parts of the poem that strike you or that you are unclear about. Look up any words you don't know.

Discuss:

1. What is the poet's attitude toward the main characters: Mary, Warren, and Silas? How do you know?

2. What is the tone of the poem? How would you describe the author's voice?

Apply:

Write two paragraphs about a public figure: someone from the world of sports, music, film, or politics. Your first paragraph should capture an admiring and approving attitude toward the public figure; your second paragraph should capture a critical and disdainful attitude toward the same public figure. As you write, don't explain your attitude. Instead, let the character's speech and actions reveal your attitude.

Frost: Lesson One

Consider:

"Silas has better claim on us you think
Than on his brother? Thirteen **little miles**
As the road winds would bring him to his door."   [Warren is speaking]

Discuss:

1. Why does Warren call the distance to Silas' brother's house 13 *little* miles? Thirteen miles is a good distance to walk. What does the diction reveal about Warren's attitude toward taking Silas in?

2. Find three or four other examples of diction that reveal a character's attitude. Share these examples in a class discussion.

Apply:

Think of something overwhelming—a school assignment you don't want to do or a gathering you don't want to attend but have to. Now write a sentence using precise diction to convey a negative attitude toward this overwhelming task. Try capturing the attitude by stating something positive, used ironically, as Frost does. Use Frost's sentence as a model.

Frost: Lesson Two

Consider:

"... You must go in and see what you can do.
I made the bed up for him there to-night.
You'll be surprised at him—how much he's **broken**.
His working days are done; I'm sure of it."   [Mary is speaking]

Discuss:

1. What effect does the use of the word *broken* have on the reader?

2. Complete the chart below, indicating how the substitution of another word for broken would change the meaning of the lines.

New word	How it would change the meaning of the lines
changed	
deteriorated	
declined	
weakened	

Apply:

Think of a place you visited as a child and then revisited as a young adult. List the ways your perception of the place has changed. Now write two (or more) lines of poetry that capture these essential changes. Choose words that are clear, concrete, and exact. You can write in blank verse, as Frost does, or in free verse.

Frost: Lesson One

Consider:

> Mary sat musing on the lamp-flame at the table
> Waiting for Warren. When she heard his step,
> She ran on tip-toe down the darkened passage
> To meet him in the doorway with the news
> And put him on his guard. "Silas is back."

Discuss:

1. What do the details in this passage reveal about Mary's attitude toward Warren?

2. How do the details prepare you for the announcement in the final line?

Apply:

Think about a time you had to announce something you didn't want to reveal. Perhaps you got a bad grade on a test or put a serious dent in your car. Write a paragraph, using concrete, specific details, to describe your actions leading up to your announcement. End your paragraph with the announcement. Share your paragraph with a partner.

Detail

Frost: Lesson Two

Consider:

"He [Silas] thinks if he could have another chance
To teach him [Harold Wilson] how to build a load of hay——" [Mary is speaking]

"I know, that's Silas' one accomplishment.
He bundles every forkful in its place,
And tags and numbers it for future reference,
So he can find and easily dislodge it
In the unloading. Silas does that well.
He takes it out in bunches like big birds' nests.
You never see him standing on the hay
He's trying to lift, straining to lift himself." [Warren is speaking]

"He thinks if he could teach him that, he'd be
Some good perhaps to someone in the world. . . ." [Mary is speaking]

Discuss:

1. What does the detail in this passage show about Silas' character?

2. What is Mary's attitude toward Silas? What is Warren's attitude toward Silas? How does the detail in this passage bring the reader into the scene and clarify the differences in attitude held by the two characters?

Apply:

Think about someone you know who is skilled or accomplished at doing something difficult. Write a sentence that clearly states the accomplishment. Use specific details—facts, observations, examples—to bring the reader into the scene and make the skill or accomplishment come alive. Use Frost's description of Silas' building a load of hay as a model.

Figurative Language

Frost: Lesson One

Consider:

"Of course he's nothing to us, any more
Than was the hound that came a stranger to us
Out of the woods, worn out upon the trail."   [Mary is speaking]

Discuss:

1. What type of figurative language is used in this passage? What are the literal and figurative terms?

2. How does this figure of speech help the reader understand the conflict of the poem?

Apply:

Write a simile or metaphor that compares a person you admire to a domesticated or wild animal. Extend your figure of speech as Frost does.

Figurative Language
Frost: Lesson Two

Consider:

"I'll sit and see if that small sailing cloud
Will hit or miss the moon."   [Mary is speaking]

It hit the moon.
Then there were three there, making a dim row,
The moon, the little silver cloud, and she.

Discuss:

1. Frost creates a strong visual image of the moon and a cloud in this passage.
   But the moon and the cloud also have symbolic value. What do the moon and the
   cloud symbolize?

2. How does the use of symbolism help the reader understand the inevitability of
   Silas' death?

Apply:

Write a description of a character in an outdoor scene you know well. Focus on one aspect
of the scene (snow, brilliant sunshine, the ocean, a river, trees, a storm, etc.). Give the
focus of your scene symbolic value by associating it with the character and the situation.
Of course, the character and situation can be triumphant rather than sad. Use Frost's
passage as a model. Share your description with another student.

Frost: Lesson One

Consider:

> Part of a moon was falling down the west,
> Dragging the whole sky with it to the hills.
> Its light poured softly in her lap. She saw it
> And spread her apron to it. She put out her hand
> Among the harp-like morning-glory strings,
> Taut with the dew from garden bed to eaves,
> As if she played unheard some tenderness
> That wrought on him beside her in the night.
> "Warren," she said, "he has come home to die:
> You needn't be afraid he'll leave you this time."

Discuss:

1. Identify the visual, auditory, and tactile images in the lines above.

2. How does Frost use imagery to prepare the reader for the revelation in the last two lines in this passage?

Apply:

Write a two-sentence description of some element in a garden or park. Be certain your sentence contains both a visual and a tactile image. Share your sentence with a partner.

 Imagery

Frost: Lesson Two

Consider:

> "I should have called it [home]
> Something you somehow haven't to deserve." [Mary is speaking]
>
> Warren leaned out and took a step or two,
> Picked up a little stick, and brought it back
> And broke it in his hand and tossed it by.

Discuss:

1. What kind of imagery is used in this passage? How does the image of Warren and the little stick help reveal Warren's attitude toward Silas' return?

2. How does the imagery in this passage contribute to the mood of the poem?

Apply:

Write two sentences that create an ominous mood of impending change. In your sentences, don't explain what is coming; instead, use a visual or auditory image to create the mood. Share your sentences with the class.

Syntax

Frost: Lesson One

Consider:

"Poor Silas, so concerned for other folk,
And nothing to look backward to with pride,
And nothing to look forward to with hope,
So now and never any different."

[Mary is speaking]

Discuss:

1. Although this passage is punctuated like a sentence, it is not a complete sentence. (There is no verb.) Instead, it is a collection of adjectives, prepositional phrases, and infinitive phrases. What effect does this use of a long sentence fragment have on the tone of the passage?

2. How would it change the impact of the passage if it were written like this?

   Poor Silas. He is always concerned for other folk.
   He has nothing to look backward to with pride.
   He has nothing to look forward to with hope.
   It's always been that way and still is.

Apply:

Think about an animal that looks pathetic or sad. It can be an animal you have seen in a zoo, in your neighborhood, or on TV. Using Frost's lines as a model, complete the frame below describing this animal in a long sentence fragment.

Poor _____, so _____ for _____,

And nothing to _____,

And nothing to _____,

So now and never any different.

Syntax

Frost: Lesson Two

Consider:

"But, Warren, please remember how it is:
He's come to help you ditch the meadow.
He has a plan. You mustn't laugh at him."   [Mary is speaking]

Discuss:

1. What is the purpose of the colon in the first sentence?

2. Notice that the first two lines contain one sentence. The third line, however, contains two short sentences. What effect does the variety in sentence length have on meaning of the passage?

Apply:

Write a long sentence that contains a polite command and an explanation of the reason behind the command. Use a colon to follow the command and give weight to the explanation. Your audience is someone just learning to do something (like solving a math problem, writing an essay, hitting a baseball, or performing a dance routine). Use the first sentence above as a model. Share your sentence with a partner.

Tone

Frost: Lesson Two

Consider:

Think about Frost's voice and tone in this poem. Read the poem again, examining how Frost uses the elements of voice to develop the tone and express his voice. Now that you have looked more deeply into the way the poem is crafted, answer the discussion questions again to see if your understanding of Frost's attitude, tone, and voice has changed.

Discuss:

1. What is Frost's attitude toward the main characters: Mary, Warren, and Silas? How do you know?

2. What is the tone of the poem? How would you describe the author's voice?

Apply:

Write a brief essay analyzing the meaning of Frost's poem and <u>how</u> meaning is conveyed. Consider the elements of voice and how they contribute to both tone and meaning. Use textual support as evidence for your analysis.

Your Turn

Frost: Culminating Lesson

Consider:

Think about Frost's poem and how he creates his tone and voice. Now write an essay or poem of your own on the topic of **home** or **homecoming**. In this essay or poem, you will develop your own tone and express your own voice.

Discuss:

1. What is the thesis or theme of your essay or poem?

2. How will you express your tone and voice using diction, detail, figurative language, imagery, and syntax?

Apply:

Write an essay or poem on home or a homecoming. Approach it any way you like, but be consistent and clear. Be certain you use all of the elements of voice to shape your tone and express your voice.

Discussion Suggestions

Robert Frost,
"The Death of the Hired Man," *North of Boston*

Tone: Lesson One

1. I have split the tone lessons so that students can see how a close analysis of a difficult text increases their understanding of both tone and voice. Tone: Lesson Two repeats the questions of Lesson One to see how students have grown in understanding of the ways authors build tone and express voice. This question stresses the importance of attitude as a determiner of tone and voice. In discussing this question with students, I suggest that you accept all answers and write them on a chart without judgment. You can then compare their answers after students have experienced the lessons about the other elements of voice.

2. Here it is important that students understand the difference between tone and voice. Tone is the author's attitude toward his or her subject or audience. Voice is the personality of the author, as revealed through his or her use of the elements of voice. They are often closely related but not always. Again, in this lesson, I suggest that you accept all answers and write them on a chart without judgment. You can then compare answers after students have experienced the lessons about the other elements of voice.

Diction: Lesson One

1. Using the word *little* to describe the 13-mile walk to his brother's house dismisses any potential objection Mary or Silas might make to Silas' going to his brother. It diminishes the distance and makes it insignificant. The diction reveals Warren's initial objection to taking Silas in and his belief that it is Silas' brother's job, not his.

2. There are many examples throughout the poem of words that reveal a character's attitude. Have students note examples, and then brainstorm and chart the words and the attitudes the words reveal.

Diction: Lesson Two

1. The word *broken* has the connotation of both physical and mental damage. It helps the reader to visualize Silas as a man in extreme physical decline and mental disarray. Silas is not merely sick or tired. He is broken, defeated, and ruined. It carries with it the feeling of total collapse.

2. Students' answers should look something like the chart on page 134.

New word	How it would change the meaning of the lines
changed	It weakens the meaning. *Changed* could have a positive or negative connotation. The lines would no longer give the reader a precise understanding of Silas' condition.
deteriorated	This word is not as strong as *broken*. Silas' condition could have gotten worse, but there is not the finality and total ruin of the word *broken*.
declined	This word, like *deteriorated*, lacks the totality and ruin of the word *broken*. Decline is a natural, even gentle, process. It happens to everyone. *Broken*, on the other hand, is active and harsh, implying an agent: time, circumstance, personal weakness, rejection.
weakened	The word *weakened* lacks precision and power. It simply implies that Silas has become sick or feeble, not that the end is in sight.

Detail: Lesson One

1. The details in this passage set the stage for the rest of the poem. Mary is *waiting* for Warren. She runs *on tip-toe* when she hears him, the passage she runs through is *darkened*, and she puts him *on his guard*. These details reveal a relationship of long-standing acceptance. Mary *gets* Warren. She knows that he will come around, but she also knows she will have to prepare him for the news, let him vent his disapproval, and calm him down. She tip-toes to him, an indication of her care and caution. The passage is dark, stressing the possible pitfalls of the discussion to come; and she puts him on his guard, showing that she must prepare him (and the reader) for the discussion to follow.

2. Although the reader does not yet know that Silas has come back to die, the details create a mood of impending doom. We know the news will not be good since Mary is waiting and thinking. She runs quietly to meet Warren and prepares him with the abrupt and terse statement, *"Silas is back,"* complete with its hint of an unwelcome reception.

Detail: Lesson Two

1. The details in this passage show Silas to be a careful worker, precise and skilled. Details also set up a personal and positive side of Silas: that he wants to share his skill with a younger man. Although this desire to share and teach is misguided, the details here still reveal a caring, proud, and helpful side to Silas' character.

2. Mary's attitude toward Silas is compassionate; she validates his good qualities and tries to stress these qualities to Warren. Warren's attitude toward Silas is one of grudging respect for his skill as a farm hand, admiration for his ability to build a load of hay, not an understanding of Silas' character. Although Warren later reveals a more sympathetic attitude toward Silas, this passage stresses the differences in attitude. The details allow the reader to eavesdrop on the conversation and fully understand the different attitudes Mary and Warren have toward Silas.

Figurative Language: Lesson One

1. There is a simile in this passage. The literal term is *he*, Silas. The figurative term is *the hound that came a stranger to us / Out of the woods, worn out upon the trail*. It is a simile because it is directly stated, using the explicit comparative phrase, *any more than*.

2. The conflict in the poem centers on the return of Silas and whether or not to take him in this time. The simile sets up Mary's argument to take Silas in. Although she says Silas is nothing more than a stray dog to them, she couches the simile in such a way as to create sympathy for the hound and thus for Silas. The hound came *out of the woods, worn out upon the trail*, indicating much suffering. In the same way, Silas has returned, broken and exhausted. Mary advocates taking Silas in just as they, presumably, took in the hound.

Figurative Language: Lesson Two

1. The moon is a traditional symbol of the feminine principle, associated with nurturing and birth. It is also a traditional symbol for the phases of life: infancy, maturity, and death. Here the moon symbolizes Mary's point of view, the traditional feminine, with its sympathy and acceptance. It also represents the phases of life, especially in conjunction with the cloud. Just as the cloud hits the moon, Silas dies; Silas reaches the final stage of life.

2. The symbolism of this passage prepares the reader for the inevitability of Silas' death and helps the reader view it with both sympathy and practicality. Just as the cloud *hits* the moon without disaster or misfortune, so Silas' death is viewed as natural. And the moon is covered by a *little silver cloud*, not a dark, menacing one. Death here is natural: sad but not frightening, inevitable but not alarming.

Imagery: Lesson One

1. A chart facilitates the examination of imagery. Images include:

Visual	Auditory	Tactile
Part of a moon was falling down the west, / Dragging the whole sky with it to the hills . . . light poured softly in her lap. She saw it / And spread her apron to it. She put out her hand / Among the harp-like morning-glory strings, / Taut with the dew from garden bed to eaves	As if she played unheard some tenderness / That wrought on him beside her in the night.	. . . light poured softly in her lap. She . . . spread her apron to it. She put out her hand / Among the harp-like morning-glory strings, / Taut with the dew from garden bed to eaves

2. The poet prepares the reader for the announcement in the last two lines of this passage by weaving a background of gentle images that center on the woman and prepare her to make her proclamation. The light from the moon *pour[s] softly in her lap*, offering comfort; and she welcomes it with her apron. She also utilizes the *morning-glory strings* to play *tenderness*, preparing Warren for her announcement. The simple, gentle ambience of the scene allows Warren to accept the impending death in the same way the woman accepts the moon's light and spreads her apron to it.

Imagery: Lesson Two

1. The imagery here is visual. The reader "sees" Warren pick up a small stick, break it, and throw it away. This image clearly reveals Warren's attitude toward Silas' return. First, it is a delay tactic, expressing some concern and allowing Warren to process the situation and determine a response. Second, the image hints at Warren's wish for the situation with Silas to be resolved, finally and absolutely, like tossing away a broken stick. Finally, the image hints at the resolution to come, one Warren suspects but cannot acknowledge directly.

2. Mood is the emotional atmosphere of a work of literature. In this poem, the mood is sad but not maudlin or mawkish. The image of Warren and his little stick helps set this mood. Although Silas dies and there is regret, the image helps the reader know that Mary and Warren will go on with their lives in a matter-of-fact and unsentimental way.

Syntax: Lesson One

1. These four lines are not a sentence—there is no main verb. There are infinitives, which are verb forms (*to look backward to, to look forward to*); however, infinitives only function as nouns, adjectives, or adverbs in sentences. Here the infinitive phrases are adjectives, modifying *nothing*. *With pride* and *with hope* are prepositional phrases. Other adjectives include *poor*, modifying *Silas; concerned*, also modifying *Silas; other*, modifying *folk*; and *different*, modifying *nothing*. Using a long sentence fragment creates an informal and conversational tone. It makes the characters come to life and makes the poem ring with authenticity. This is the way Mary speaks. You can hear her voice, complete with its matter-of-fact sadness.

2. The changed passage sounds choppy, mechanical, and stiff. It has none of the realistic pacing of a natural conversational style. It no longer sounds like Mary.

Syntax: Lesson Two

1. The colon in the first sentence shifts the reader's attention and emphasizes the words that follow the colon. Here, Mary is emphasizing the importance of leaving Silas with some remnant of self-respect. Of course, Mary knows that Silas' coming back to work is not *how it is*; but she is urging Warren to recognize the importance of Silas' dignity.

2. The long sentence of the first two lines in this passage prepares the reader for what follows. Short sentences usually carry the most important information in English, and that holds true in this passage. Silas *has a plan*, an unequivocal statement directed at Warren with an understood directive not to embarrass Silas. The final sentence, *You mustn't laugh at him*, is both a command and a plea. The sentence sums

up, in one brief, direct, short sentence, Mary's concern for Silas and her urgent appeal to Warren's basic decency to leave Silas' self-respect intact.

Tone: Lesson Two

1. I have split the tone lessons so that students can see how a close analysis of a difficult text increases their understanding of both tone and voice. This lesson repeats the questions of Tone: Lesson One to see how students have grown in understanding of the ways authors build tone and express voice. The question stresses the importance of attitude as a determiner of tone and voice. The poet's <u>attitude</u> toward the three main characters is sympathetic and positive. Mary is the chief advocate for compassion. She asks Warren to *be kind* and urges him not to *grudge the poor old man / Some humble way to save his self-respect*. She notes Silas' strength (*Poor Silas, so concerned for other folk*) and urges Warren not to laugh at him. Warren, although resistant to taking Silas in initially, also understands compassion. He recognizes Silas' skill with haying and finally admits Silas' good nature: *I can't think Si ever hurt anyone* and goes to see him. The attitude toward Silas is complicated. There is a poignancy in his return to Warren and Mary. He is not looking for charity; he has a plan: to work, to teach a younger man how to load hay, to make the farm better for Mary and Warren. Of course, he is unable to do any of these things, but he resists Mary's help (*he wouldn't let me put him on the lounge*) and wants to work. His lack of self-awareness (*He don't know why he isn't quite as good / As anyone*) and his awkward pride (*He won't be made ashamed / To please his brother, worthless though he is*) make him a sad but noble character.

Attitude is revealed through the diction, choice of details, images, figurative language, and syntax.

Any similar answers are acceptable as long as students support their answers with evidence from the text. As students discuss these questions again, take notes on a large chart. Compare this chart with the chart you developed with students at the beginning of this section. Lead a discussion about the ways close analysis of a piece of writing deepens with knowledge of the elements of voice.

2. Review the difference between tone and voice with your students. Tone is the author's attitude toward his or her subject or audience. Voice is the personality of the author, as revealed through his or her use of the elements of voice. Here the tone and voice are essentially the same, but that is not always true. Students may express different answers to these questions. Their answers are acceptable, of course, if they can support their answers with evidence from the text. Frost's tone in this essay is respectful and sympathetic. The poem captures the difficulty of the situation (Warren complains, *Off he goes always when I need him most*) and the nobility of the characters as they respond to each other. His voice is objective (he describes the characters without explanation or embellishment), insightful, and ultimately sympathetic (he clearly finds something to admire in all of the characters). As in Question 1, take notes on a chart while students discuss these questions. Compare this chart with the one you developed with students at the beginning of this section. Lead a discussion about the ways close analysis of a piece of writing deepens with knowledge of the elements of voice.

Your Turn: Culminating Lesson

1. If students have trouble deciding on a focused topic or theme, it would be helpful to take some time to guide them in ways (modeling, brainstorming, graphic organizers, freewriting) to find a compelling topic or theme, narrow their approach, and gather ideas. It would also be helpful to give students quiet time to think and then time to discuss ideas in pairs or small groups. Ultimately, students will have to decide on their own themes and how they will develop them; but support and guidance never hurt. What they decide will determine their tone and help shape their voice. Students should jot down their themes and some ideas about development to keep in mind as they draft their essays or poems.

2. Students will also have to decide the tone they want to develop in their essays or poems. By now they should understand that they have the power to craft a specific tone through focused use of the elements of voice. If they keep a specific tone in mind, they will shape their essays or poems in ways that reveal their tone to their readers. Voice is individual and distinctive. Will their essays or poems be passionate? Cool and studied? Humorous? Balanced and rational? Positive? Negative? For this assignment, students should have the freedom to develop their own voices through the skillful use of the elements of voice.

President John F. Kennedy, from Remarks at Amherst College
(October 26, 1963)

This day devoted to the memory of Robert Frost offers an opportunity for reflection which is prized by politicians as well as by others, and even by poets, for Robert Frost was one of the granite figures of our time in America. He was supremely two things: an artist and an American. A nation reveals itself not only by the men it produces but also by the men it honors, the men it remembers.

In America, our heroes have customarily run to men of large accomplishments. But today this college and country honors a man whose contribution was not to our size but to our spirit, not to our political beliefs but to our insight, not to our self-esteem, but to our self-comprehension. In honoring Robert Frost, we therefore can pay honor to the deepest sources of our national strength. That strength takes many forms, and the most obvious forms are not always the most significant. The men who create power make an indispensable contribution to the Nation's greatness, but the men who question power make a contribution just as indispensable, especially when that questioning is disinterested, for they determine whether we use power or power uses us.

Our national strength matters, but the spirit which informs and controls our strength matters just as much. This was the special significance of Robert Frost. He brought an unsparing instinct for reality to bear on the platitudes and pieties of society. His sense of the human tragedy fortified him against self-deception and easy consolation. "I have been," he wrote, "one acquainted with the night." And because he knew the midnight as well as the high noon, because he understood the ordeal as well as the triumph of the human spirit, he gave his age strength with which to overcome despair. At bottom, he held a deep faith in the spirit of man, and it is hardly an accident that Robert Frost coupled poetry and power, for he saw poetry as the means of saving power from itself. When power leads man towards arrogance, poetry reminds him of his limitations. When power narrows the areas of man's concern, poetry reminds him of the richness and diversity of his existence. When power corrupts, poetry cleanses. For art establishes the basic human truth which must serve as the touchstone of our judgment.

The artist, however faithful to his personal vision of reality, becomes the last champion of the individual mind and sensibility against an intrusive society and an officious state. The great artist is thus a solitary figure. He has, as Frost said, a lover's quarrel with the world. In pursuing his perceptions of reality, he must often sail against the currents of his time. This is not a popular role. If Robert Frost was much honored during his lifetime, it was because a good many preferred to ignore his darker truths. Yet in retrospect, we see how the artist's fidelity has strengthened the fibre of our national life.

If sometimes our great artists have been the most critical of our society, it is because their sensitivity and their concern for justice, which must motivate any true artist, makes him aware that our Nation falls short of its highest potential. I see little of more importance to the future of our country and our civilization than full recognition of the place of the artist.

If art is to nourish the roots of our culture, society must set the artist free to follow his vision wherever it takes him. We must never forget that art is not a form of propaganda; it is a form of truth. And as Mr. MacLeish once remarked of poets, there is nothing worse for our trade than to be in style. In free society art is not a weapon and it does not belong to the sphere of polemics and ideology. Artists are not engineers of the soul. It may be different elsewhere. But democratic society—in it, the highest duty of the writer, the composer, the artist is to remain true to himself and to let the chips fall where they may. In serving his vision of the truth, the artist best serves his nation. And the nation which disdains the mission of art invites the fate of Robert Frost's hired man, the fate of having "nothing to look backward to with pride, and nothing to look forward to with hope."

I look forward to a great future for America, a future in which our country will match its military strength with our moral restraint, its wealth with our wisdom, its power with our purpose. I look forward to an America which will not be afraid of grace and beauty, which will protect the beauty of our natural environment, which will preserve the great old American houses and squares and parks of our national past, and which will build handsome and balanced cities for our future.

I look forward to an America which will reward achievement in the arts as we reward achievement in business or statecraft. I look forward to an America which will steadily raise the standards of artistic accomplishment and which will steadily enlarge cultural opportunities for all of our citizens. And I look forward to an America which commands respect throughout the world not only for its strength but for its civilization as well. And I look forward to a world which will be safe not only for democracy and diversity but also for personal distinction.

Robert Frost was often skeptical about projects for human improvement, yet I do not think he would disdain this hope. As he wrote during the uncertain days of the Second War:

> Take human nature altogether since time began . . .
> And it must be a little more in favor of man,
> Say a fraction of one percent at the very least . . .
> Our hold on the planet wouldn't have so increased."

Because of Mr. Frost's life and work, because of the life and work of this college, our hold on this planet has increased.

To the Student:

♣ John F. Kennedy was the 35th president of the United States. Well educated and articulate, his speeches still ring with urgency and depth. This speech, delivered in 1963, is both a tribute to Robert Frost and an affirmation of the importance of great artists in our society. The language of the speech should offer no difficulties, but the thoughts are rich and complex. Read the speech with care. Even better, read the speech **aloud** with care. The language is both graceful and forceful and should be read aloud with conviction. Please note that President Kennedy refers to all people as *men* or *he*. This follows the grammatical convention of the time and is not intended to demean the importance of women.

Tone

President Kennedy: Lesson One

Consider:

Read the speech several times slowly and carefully. Use underlining or highlighting and marginal notes to help you clarify parts of the speech you wonder about. Look up any words you do not know and mark parts of the speech you find particularly compelling.

Discuss:

1. Identify the purpose and thesis of this speech. Who is the audience?

2. What is the tone of the speech? How would you describe the author's voice?

Apply:

Write a paragraph or two about the importance of the artist (musician, film director, writer, dancer, and so on) in our culture. Create a tone of self-confidence and certainty. Express your own ideas. You don't, of course, have to agree with Kennedy.

President Kennedy: Lesson One

Consider:

He brought an **unsparing** instinct for reality to bear on the **platitudes** and **pieties** of society.

Discuss:

1. Look up the three boldface words in the passage above and be certain you understand their meaning. Explain how each word clearly and exactly expresses President Kennedy's opinion of Frost.

2. Do the words *platitudes* and *pieties* have a negative or positive connotation in this passage? How do you know?

Apply:

Complete the following sentence frame with words that are clear, concrete, and exact. Your sentence should describe a man or woman you admire.

He/She brought a(n) _____ belief in

to bear on the _____ and _____ of

_____.

President Kennedy: Lesson Two

Consider:

The artist, however faithful to his personal vision of reality, becomes the last **champion** of the individual mind and sensibility against an **intrusive society and an officious state**.

Discuss:

1. The word *champion* does not mean *winner* in this sentence. What does it mean? What effect does the use of the word *champion* have on the reader?

2. Why do you think President Kennedy calls society potentially *intrusive* and the state potentially *officious*? What does Kennedy's diction reveal about his view of the role of the artist in society?

Apply:

Write an original sentence using the word *champion* in the same way that Kennedy does. Use Kennedy's sentence as a model. Share your sentence with a partner.

Detail

President Kennedy: Lesson One

Consider:

In free society art is not a weapon and it does not belong to the sphere of polemics and ideology. Artists are not engineers of the soul. It may be different elsewhere. But democratic society—in it, the highest duty of the writer, the composer, the artist is to remain true to himself and to let the chips fall where they may. In serving his vision of the truth, the artist best serves his nation.

Discuss:

1. What is President Kennedy's assertion in this passage? What details support this assertion?

2. How does Kennedy's use of detail help shape the tone of the speech?

Apply:

Write a paragraph filled with details that support this assertion: A good student is not one who repeats what he or she thinks the teacher wants to hear.

Detail

President Kennedy: Lesson Two

Consider:

I look forward to an America which will not be afraid of grace and beauty, which will protect the beauty of our natural environment, which will preserve the great old American houses and squares and parks of our national past, and which will build handsome and balanced cities for our future.

Discuss:

1. How does the use of detail in this passage narrow and define what President Kennedy means by *grace and beauty*?

2. How would it change the reader's understanding of Kennedy's attitude if the passage were written like this?

   I look forward to an America which will not be afraid of grace and beauty, which will respect nature and all of the things that the people of this country have made.

Apply:

Define a good school, using specific details to develop and support your definition. Share your definition and details with your class.

Figurative Language

President Kennedy: Lesson One

Consider:

Robert Frost was one of the granite figures of our time in America.

Discuss:

1. Identify the figure of speech in the sentence above. What are the literal and figurative terms?

2. What insight does the figure of speech give into Frost's importance in American culture? Why do you think President Kennedy used a figure of speech rather than just saying Robert Frost was a great man?

Apply:

Write a metaphor that gives insight into someone you admire. Don't explain your admiration; instead, let the metaphor work for you, providing multiple meanings and precision of expression.

Figurative Language
President Kennedy: Lesson Two

Consider:

I see little of more importance to the future of our country and our civilization than full recognition of the place of the artist. If art is to nourish the roots of our culture, society must set the artist free to follow his vision wherever it takes him.

Discuss:

1. President Kennedy uses a metaphor to define the purpose of art. Identify the metaphor and its literal and figurative terms.

2. How would it change the impact of these lines if Kennedy had said this?

   If art is to shape our cultural values, society must set the artist free to follow his vision wherever it takes him.

Apply:

Write a metaphor that captures the importance of exercise to good health. For example, you could say that exercise is a ladder to good health. Now write a complete sentence using the metaphor to define the purpose of exercise and extending the idea of the connection between health and exercise. You can start with this example or use Kennedy's sentence as a model for expressing your own ideas.

President Kennedy: Lesson One

Consider:

"I have been," he [Frost] wrote, "one acquainted with the night." And because he knew the midnight as well as the high noon, because he understood the ordeal as well as the triumph of the human spirit, he gave his age strength with which to overcome despair.

Discuss:

1. What kind of imagery is used in this passage? How does the use of imagery help shape the reader's understanding of Frost's contribution to our society?

2. Remember that imagery can also be figurative. This passage contains examples of metaphor and metonymy that are also images. Identify the figures of speech and explain how they help shape the tone of the passage.

Apply:

Think of something or someone you genuinely like. It could be a sport, a book, a kind of food, a person—something or someone you know well and have strong feelings about. Describe what you have chosen with an image that is also a metaphor. Share your description with a partner.

President Kennedy: Lesson Two

Consider:

The great artist is thus a solitary figure. He has, as Frost said, a lover's quarrel with the world. In pursuing his perceptions of reality, he must often sail against the currents of his time. This is not a popular role.

Discuss:

1. Describe the image this passage creates in your mind. How does this image help you fully understand President Kennedy's view of the artist?

2. The image in the first sentence is not figurative, but in the third sentence the imagery is figurative. Analyze the images in those two sentences and explain the effect that literal and figurative imagery has on the reader.

Apply:

Using Kennedy's passage as a model, describe a great athlete, a great friend, or a great leader. Your description should include a literal image and a figurative one.

Syntax

President Kennedy: Lesson One

Consider:

In America, our heroes have customarily run to men of large accomplishments. But today this college and country honors a man whose contribution was not to our size but to our spirit, not to our political beliefs but to our insight, not to our self-esteem, but to our self-comprehension.

Discuss:

1. Notice that President Kennedy starts the second sentence with a conjunction, *but*. You may have been taught not to do that; however, there is really no reason we can't start sentences with conjunctions in English (in moderation). What is the purpose of starting the sentence with a conjunction, and how does it direct the reader's attention to the words that follow?

2. Kennedy uses the word *but* three more times in the sentence. What effect does this continued use of the conjunction have on the tone of the passage?

Apply:

Write a sentence that starts with a conjunction and expresses a contrasting idea to the following sentence: *In school, students are often judged by how well they do on standardized tests.* Share your sentence with the class.

Syntax

President Kennedy: Lesson Two

Consider:

I look forward to a great future for America, a future in which our country will match its military strength with our moral restraint, its wealth with our wisdom, its power with our purpose. I look forward to an America which will not be afraid of grace and beauty, which will protect the beauty of our natural environment, which will preserve the great old American houses and squares and parks of our national past, and which will build handsome and balanced cities for our future.

I look forward to an America which will reward achievement in the arts as we reward achievement in business or statecraft. I look forward to an America which will steadily raise the standards of artistic accomplishment and which will steadily enlarge cultural opportunities for all of our citizens. And I look forward to an America which commands respect throughout the world not only for its strength but for its civilization as well. And I look forward to a world which will be safe not only for democracy and diversity but also for personal distinction.

Discuss:

1. In the passage above, President Kennedy repeats the phrase *I look forward to* six times. This is called anaphora, the deliberate repetition of the first part of a sentence. What effect does the use of anaphora have on the reader?

2. In what other ways does Kennedy use repetition in these paragraphs? How does the use of repetition reinforce meaning?

Apply:

Think about your idea of a perfect vacation. What would you look forward to and what would you want to happen? Write a paragraph using anaphora and other forms of repetition in order to draw attention to and emphasize your ideas. Use Kennedy's paragraphs as a model. Share your paragraph with a partner.

Tone

President Kennedy: Lesson Two

Consider:

Think about President Kennedy's voice, his tone in this speech, and how he uses the elements of voice to accomplish his purpose. Now that you have looked more deeply into the way the speech is crafted, answer the discussion questions again to see if your understanding of the author's purpose, thesis, tone, and voice has changed.

Discuss:

1. Identify the purpose and thesis of the speech.

2. What is the tone of the speech? How would you describe the author's voice?

Apply:

Write a brief essay analyzing the meaning and purpose of Kennedy's speech and how meaning is conveyed. Consider the elements of voice and how they contribute to both purpose and meaning. Use textual support as evidence for your analysis.

Your Turn

President Kennedy: Culminating Lesson

Consider:

Think about President Kennedy's speech and how he creates his tone and voice. Now write a speech of your own on the importance of music (or art, or dance, or sports, or gaming) in society. In this speech, you will develop your own tone and express your own voice.

Discuss:

1. Identify the purpose and thesis of your speech? Who is your audience?

2. How will you express your tone and voice using diction, detail, figurative language, imagery, and syntax?

Apply:

Write a speech on the importance of music (or art, or dance, or sports, or video gaming) in society. Approach it any way you like, but be consistent and clear. Be certain you use all of the elements of voice to shape your tone and express your voice. Deliver your speech to the class.

Discussion Suggestions

President John F. Kennedy, from Remarks at Amherst College
(October 26, 1963)

Tone: Lesson One

1. I have split the tone lessons so that students can see how a close analysis of a complex text increases their understanding of both tone and voice. Tone: Lesson Two repeats the questions of Lesson One to see how students have grown in understanding of the ways authors build tone and express voice. This question stresses the importance of purpose, audience, and thesis, or main idea, as determiners of tone and voice. In discussing this question with students, I suggest that you accept all answers and write them on a chart without judgment. You can then compare their answers after students have experienced the lessons about the other elements of voice.

2. Here it is important that students understand the difference between tone and voice. Tone is the author's attitude toward his or her subject or audience. Voice is the personality of the author, as revealed through his or her use of the elements of voice. They are often closely related but not always. Again, in this lesson, I suggest that you accept all answers and write them on a chart without judgment. You can then compare answers after students have experienced the lessons about the other elements of voice.

Diction: Lesson One

1. The word *unsparing* means unrelenting. It captures what President Kennedy wants us to understand about Frost's *instinct for reality*. In other words, Frost spared no words as he described reality as he saw it. The *platitudes and pieties of society* perfectly describe the banalities and hypocrisy of society, a society that clearly needs Frost's *unsparing instinct for reality*.

2. Both words have a negative connotation in this passage. This is clear since they are put in direct contrast to Frost's *unsparing instinct for reality*. They are something to be corrected not extolled.

Diction: Lesson Two

1. *Champion* in this context means a defender or supporter. Here, the artist is a defender of *the individual mind and sensibility*. The effect on the reader is to evoke a vision of the artist as a kind of Don Quixote of individualism, a standard-bearer of the rights and importance of independent thinking. The reader understands the artist as a safeguard against potential abuses of government.

2. Both words, *intrusive* and *officious*, mean meddling, invasive, and interfering. Kennedy is exploring the dangers of a government that is not checked by the spirit of the artist. The artist, by his or her vision and defense of the individual, holds government at bay and keeps the essence of freedom alive. The artist, then, is the guardian of freedom and the consummate social critic, reminding all people to stand up against hypocrisy and a government that oversteps its bounds.

Detail: Lesson One

1. President Kennedy's assertion is that the artist's duty is to serve his or her vision of the truth. The details he uses are reasons and observations that support his assertion. Details include the following quotes:

   - *In free society art is not a weapon . . .*
   - *. . . it [art] does not belong to the sphere of polemics and ideology.*
   - *Artists are not engineers of the soul.*
   - *. . . the highest duty of the writer, the composer, the artist is to remain true to himself . . .*
   - *In serving his vision of truth, the artist best serves his nation.*

2. Kennedy's use of detail in this passage reinforces the tone of the speech that has already been established. Kennedy's tone is forceful, reverential, and self-assured. He expresses his convictions through reasons and observations, asserting that his vision of the artist is true and offering only the details that support his view. There is no equivocation or hedging here. Kennedy selects details that forcefully advocate for the truth of his assertion.

Detail: Lesson Two

1. The details in this passage that narrow and define Kennedy's view of *grace and beauty* are examples. Examples of *grace and beauty* include:

   - protecting the beauty of our natural environment.
   - preserving the great old American houses and squares and parks of our national past.
   - building handsome and balanced cities for our future.

2. The new passage has none of the eloquence and power of the original passage. The examples are abstract and vague, lending little support for what Kennedy believes about *grace and beauty*. The new passage reveals a generic and pallid attitude; it takes away any passion and certitude, qualities that mark the attitude expressed in the original passage.

Figurative Language: Lesson One

1. *Robert Frost was one of the granite figures of our time in America* is a metaphor. The literal term is *Robert Frost* and the figurative term is *granite figure*.

2. Frost was not, of course, a literal figure made of granite. Kennedy gives insight into Frost's character and contributions by comparing Frost to a granite statue. Granite is hard and durable, a stone often used in monuments and memorials. In addition, it is textured, giving it a complex and often uneven appearance. Kennedy brings all of these qualities to his tribute to Frost through a simple metaphor. Kennedy could have gone on and on, explaining how Frost was a towering figure, how he endures, how his work is complex and varied, how his poems are a memorial to the man and his age. But by calling Frost a granite figure, he says it all. He gives the reader a clear picture of Frost's character and contributions. The language is poetic and concise, and the reader understands Frost through the comparison.

Figurative Language: Lesson Two

1. The metaphor is complex, and much of it is implied. However, the comparison is apt and can be paraphrased like this: The purpose of art is to enrich the foundations of our culture [like] the purpose of soil or fertilizer is to nourish the roots of plants. The literal term is art that enriches our culture (implied). The figurative term is soil or fertilizer (implied) that nourishes the roots of plants.

2. Without the metaphor, the lines lack depth and complexity. The meaning is not changed dramatically, but the lines lose their power to engage the reader. The new lines explain rather than trusting the reader to understand. It is no longer a conversation of intellectual equals but an explanation for people of inferior understanding. In addition, the lines lose their grace and eloquence, qualities important for a memorable speech.

Imagery: Lesson One

1. The imagery in this passage is visual. President Kennedy pictures Frost and, by implication, the artist, standing in the darkness of night and in the bright light of day. The imagery helps the reader visualize and understand that Frost and great artists in general have known both the hardships and disappointments of darkness and the hope and good times of the light. These experiences shape Frost's understanding of the world and allow him to help others gain the strength to *overcome despair*.

2. The chart below gives the metaphors and their literal and figurative terms.

   The example of metonymy (and a visual image) is *he gave his age strength*. One can't literally give an *age* strength. Kennedy uses the word *age* to represent the people of Frost's time. But *age* also carries with it deeper meaning: an epoch, a historic period, people living in a certain time. By using images with figurative meaning, Kennedy intensifies the reader's understanding of the scope and importance of Frost's role in the history of thought.

Metaphor	Literal Term	Figurative Term
troubles and suffering = the night	(implied) *troubles and suffering*	*night* (the darkness of night is traditionally associated with danger and strife)
troubles and suffering = midnight	(implied) *troubles and suffering*	*midnight*
good times and hope = high noon	(implied) *good times and hope*	*high noon* (the light of day is traditionally associated with hope and good times)

Imagery: Lesson Two

1. The image President Kennedy creates is a visual one: the artist standing alone and sailing off alone against the ocean's currents. The imagery helps us understand Kennedy's view of the artist as the voice of truth, a lone voice, railing against commonly held beliefs and misconceptions.

2. The *solitary figure* gives the reader a picture of a person standing alone. It is an image but not figurative. In the third sentence, Kennedy takes the idea of a lonely figure deeper through the use of a metaphor. The artist (literal term) is someone (figurative term: a sailor) who speaks (figurative term: *sails*) against popular beliefs (figurative term: *the currents of the sea*). Both the literal and figurative imagery bring the reader into a full and rich understanding of the role of the artist in society.

Syntax: Lesson One

1. Starting the sentence with a conjunction catches the reader's attention, emphasizes the meaning of the conjunction, and forces a kind of pause or hesitation. In addition, this conjunction indicates a contrasting idea, opposition. Because it indicates an opposing idea to follow, it directs the reader's attention to the ideas that follow, those in contrast to the preceding ideas.

2. The continued use of *but* sets up a pattern of contrasts: *not to our size **but** to our spirit; not to our political beliefs **but** to our insight; not to our self-esteem, **but** to our self-comprehension*. Note the balance of the sentence. Kennedy mentions typical American heroes and their contributions (American greatness, politics, and self-esteem). He contrasts these contributions with what he considers the more significant contributions of the great artist (American spirit, insight, and self-comprehension). Setting up the pattern of contrasts reinforces the confident tone of the passage. Kennedy knows what is commonly thought; but he, like the artist, stands alone and declares what he thinks is most important.

Syntax: Lesson Two

1. Anaphora is a technique often used in speeches. It serves to emphasize the ideas that are repeated. Furthermore, the repetition functions to persuade the audience (or readers) that the speaker (or writer) speaks the truth; and it is designed to inspire others to agree with the ideas presented after the anaphora. Here the use of anaphora emphasizes Kennedy's positive stance toward the artist and the artist's role in America. The repetition serves to align the reader with Kennedy's hope for a positive future.

2. Kennedy repeats the word *future* in the first sentence of the passage (*I look forward to a great future for America, a future in which. . . .*). The repetition here emphasizes the future and what will make it great. Kennedy goes on in that sentence to repeat a series of phrases that balance what is usually thought of as great in America with the greatness the artist can offer. There are three direct objects (explaining what is usually thought of as great in America) of the verb *match*: *its military strength, **its wealth**, and *its power*. These are balanced with prepositional phrases (representing the contributions of the artist): *with our moral restraint, with our wisdom, and with our purpose*. The repetition of form serves to emphasize the need for balance.

But it is important to note that the structure also has an essential change. The usual characteristics of greatness are neutralized by the word *its*. On the other hand, when Kennedy speaks of the artist's contribution, he uses the word *our*. This change from a simple pattern of repetition to a structural pattern with change emphasizes Kennedy's affirmation of the essential role of the artist. The country needs *its* military, wealth, and power. But the *people* of the country need *our* moral restraint, wisdom, and purpose. This brings the reader into a community of thought that aligns with Kennedy's belief in the important role of the artist in society. The same pattern of repetition and affirmation echoes through the last two sentences of the passage. Both sentences start with *and*, an indication of important information to follow. Kennedy also uses a *not only . . . but also* construction to continue his plea for balance between *strength* and *civilization* and a world safe for *democracy* and *personal distinction*.

Tone: Lesson Two

1. I have split the tone lessons so that students can see how a close analysis of a complex text increases their understanding of both tone and voice. This lesson repeats the questions of Tone: Lesson One to see how students have grown in understanding of the ways authors build tone and express voice; and the question stresses the importance of purpose, audience, and thesis as determiners of tone and voice. Possible purposes for this speech include to reflect, to convince readers of the importance of art, to honor Robert Frost, and the like.

The audience, as we can infer from the diction, syntax, and tone, is a group of educated men and women. The thesis is stated in many different ways, but it is quite clearly stated in the third paragraph: *Our national strength matters, but the spirit which informs and controls our strength matters just as much.* This idea, and the connection between that spirit and art, is the central contention of the speech. Any variation of these answers is acceptable as long as students support their answers with evidence from the text. As students discuss these questions again, take notes on a large chart. Compare this chart with the chart you developed with students at the beginning of this section. Lead a discussion about the ways close analysis of a piece of writing deepens with knowledge of the elements of voice.

2. Review the difference between tone and voice with your students. Tone is the author's attitude toward his or her subject or audience. Voice is the personality of the author, as revealed through his or her use of the elements of voice. Students may express different answers to these questions. Their answers are acceptable, of course, if they can support their answers with evidence from the text. Kennedy's tone in this speech is forceful, reverential, and self-assured. His voice is confident, passionate, and strong. As in Question 1, take notes on a chart while students discuss these questions. Compare this chart with the one you developed with students at the beginning of this section. Lead a discussion about the ways close analysis of a piece of writing deepens with knowledge of the elements of voice.

Your Turn: Culminating Lesson

1. If students have trouble deciding on a specific topic or thesis, it would be helpful to take some time to guide them in ways (modeling, brainstorming, graphic organizers, freewriting) to find an important topic, narrow their approach, and gather ideas. It would also be helpful to give students quiet time to think and then time to discuss ideas in pairs or small groups. Ultimately, students will have to decide on their own topic and thesis and how they will develop them; but support and guidance never hurt. What they decide will determine their tone and help shape their voice. Students should write down their thesis and some ideas about development to keep in mind as they draft their speeches.

2. Students will also have to decide the tone they want to develop in their speeches. By now they should understand that they have the power to craft a specific tone through focused use of the elements of voice. If they keep a specific tone in mind, they will shape their speech in such a way as to reveal their tone to their readers. Voice is individual and distinctive. Will their speeches be passionate? Cool and studied? Humorous? Balanced and rational? Ironic? Positive? Negative? For this assignment, students should have the freedom to develop their own voices through the skillful use of the elements of voice.

William Shakespeare, *Hamlet*

ACT 2, SCENE 2, LINES 254–334

Enter Guildenstern and Rosencrantz

HAMLET: What news?

ROSENCRANTZ: None, my lord, but that the world's grown honest.

HAMLET: Then is doomsday near. But your news is not true. Let me question more in particular. What have you, my good friends, deserved at the hands of Fortune that she sends you to prison hither?

GUILDENSTERN: Prison, my lord?

HAMLET: Denmark's a prison.

ROSENCRANTZ: Then is the world one.

HAMLET: A goodly one, in which there are many confines, wards, and dungeons, Denmark being one o' th' worst.

ROSENCRANTZ: We think not so, my lord.

HAMLET: Why, then, 'tis none to you, for there is nothing either good or bad that thinking makes it so. To me, it is a prison.

ROSENCRANTZ: Why, then, your ambition makes it one. 'Tis too narrow for your mind.

HAMLET: O God, I could be bounded in a nutshell and count myself a king of infinite space, were it not that I have bad dreams.

GUILDENSTERN: Which dreams, indeed, are ambition, for the very substance of the ambitious is merely the shadow of a dream.

HAMLET: A dream itself is but a shadow.

ROSENCRANTZ: Truly, and I hold ambition of so airy and light a quality that it is but a shadow's shadow.

HAMLET: Then are our beggars bodies, and our monarchs and outstretched heroes the beggars' shadows. Shall we to th' court? For, by my fay, I cannot reason.

ROSENCRANTZ/
GUILDENSTERN: We'll wait upon you.

HAMLET: No such matter. I will not sort you with the rest of my servants, for, to speak to you like an honest man, I am most dreadfully attended. But, in the beaten way of friendship, what make you at Elsinore?

ROSENCRANTZ: To visit you, my lord, no other occasion.

HAMLET: Beggar that I am, I am even poor in thanks; but I thank you, and sure, dear friends, my thanks are too dear a halfpenny. Were you not sent for? Is it your own inclining? Is it a free visitation? Come, come, deal justly with me. Come, come; nay, speak.

GUILDENSTERN: What should we say, my lord?

HAMLET: Anything but to th' purpose. You were sent for, and there is a kind of confession in your looks which your modesties have not craft enough to color. I know the good king and queen have sent for you.

ROSENCRANTZ: To what end, my lord?

HAMLET: That you must teach me. But let me conjure you by the rights of our fellowship, by the consonancy of our youth, by the obligation of our ever-preserved love, and by what more dear a better proposer can charge you withal: be even and direct with me whether you were sent for or no.

ROSENCRANTZ
[TO GUILDENSTERN]: What say you?

HAMLET [ASIDE]: Nay, then, I have an eye of you.—If you love me, hold not off.

GUILDENSTERN: My lord, we were sent for.

HAMLET: I will tell you why; so shall my anticipation prevent your discovery, and your secrecy to the King and Queen molt no feather. I have of late, but wherefore I know not, lost all my mirth, forgone all custom of exercises, and, indeed, it goes so heavily with my disposition that this goodly frame, the earth, seems to me a sterile promontory; this most excellent canopy, the air, look you, this brave o'er-hanging firmament, this majestical roof, fretted with golden fire—why, it appeareth nothing to me but a foul and pestilent congregation of vapors. What a piece of work is a man, how noble in reason, how infinite in faculties, in form and moving how express and admirable; in action how like an angel, in apprehension how like a god: the beauty of the world, the paragon of animals—and yet, to me, what is this quintessence of dust? Man delights not me, no, nor women neither, though by your smiling you seem to say so.

ACT 3, SCENE 2, LINES 339–402

Enter Guildenstern and Rosencrantz.

GUILDENSTERN: The Queen your mother, in most great affliction of spirit, hath sent me to you.

HAMLET: You are welcome.

GUILDENSTERN: Nay, good my lord, this courtesy is not of the right breed. If it shall please you to make me a wholesome answer, I will do your mother's commandment. If not, your pardon and my return shall be the end of my business.

HAMLET: Sir, I cannot.

ROSENCRANTZ: What, my lord?

HAMLET: Make you a wholesome answer. My wit's diseased. But, sir, such answer as I can make, you shall command—or, rather, as you say, my mother. Therefore no more but to the matter. My mother, you say—

ROSENCRANTZ: Then thus she says: your behavior has struck her into amazement and admiration.

HAMLET: O wonderful son that can so 'stonish a mother! But is there no sequel at the heels of this mother's admiration? Impart.

ROSENCRANTZ: She desires to speak with you in her closet ere you go to bed.

HAMLET: We shall obey, were she ten times our mother. Have you any further trade with us?

ROSENCRANTZ: My lord, you once did love me.

HAMLET: And still do . . . .

ROSENCRANTZ: Good my lord, what is the cause of your distemper? You do surely bar the door upon your own liberty if you deny your griefs to your friend.

HAMLET: Sir, I lack advancement.

ROSENCRANTZ: How can that be, when you have the voice of the King himself for your succession in Denmark?

Enter the Players with recorders

HAMLET: . . . O, the recorders! Let me see one. [*He takes a recorder and turns to Guildenstern.*] . . . . Will you play upon this pipe?

GUILDENSTERN: My lord, I cannot.

HAMLET: I pray you.

GUILDENSTERN: Believe me, I cannot.

HAMLET: I do beseech you.

GUILDENSTERN: I know no touch of it, my lord.

HAMLET: It is as easy as lying. Govern these ventages with your fingers and thumb, give it breath with your mouth, and it will discourse most eloquent music. Look you, these are the stops.

GUILDENSTERN: But these I cannot command to any utt'rance of harmony. I have not the skill.

HAMLET: Why, look you now, how unworthy a thing you make of me! You would play upon me, you would seem to know my stops, you would pluck out the heart of my mystery, you would sound me from my lowest note to the top of my compass; and there is much music, excellent voice, in this little organ, yet cannot you make it speak. 'Sblood, do you think I am easier to be played on than a pipe? Call me what instrument you will, though you can fret me, you cannot play upon me.

To the Student:

♣ If you have never read or seen the play *Hamlet*, you should do so. This complex drama is intense, troubling, and timeless. It also contains some of the most beautiful language in English literary history. But if you have not read or viewed *Hamlet* and don't want to spend the time, here is a brief plot summary:

> The play begins with a difficult situation for Hamlet, a young prince of Denmark. His father (the king of Denmark) has died, his uncle Claudius has become king, and Claudius has married Hamlet's mother Gertrude. Hamlet, called home from college, has a visitation (real? true?) from his father's ghost. The ghost informs Hamlet that Claudius murdered him and seduced and married his wife. The ghost commands Hamlet to avenge the murder. Hamlet has a problem. In fact, Hamlet has several problems: Claudius, Gertrude, his girlfriend Ophelia and her family, his friends, and his father's ghost's command. It takes Hamlet the rest of the play to exact his revenge. The play does not end happily for anyone.

There are two questions in this play that readers struggle with: Why does it take so long for Hamlet to avenge his father's murder? And do his problems cause Hamlet to sink into madness? Keep these questions in mind if you read or view the play.

The two scenes quoted above from *Hamlet* portray the interaction between Hamlet and two of his old friends, Rosencrantz and Guildenstern. The friends have been summoned to court by Claudius to find out what is wrong with Hamlet, who has been acting strangely. (Claudius is afraid Hamlet is onto something and wants to find out what.) These scenes bring up the question of Hamlet's madness. More importantly for our purposes, though, is the use of language in these scenes. It is a study in how a literary genius creates tone in writing.

Tone

Shakespeare: Lesson One

Consider:

Read these scenes from *Hamlet* several times slowly and carefully. Use underlining or highlighting and marginal notes to help clarify parts of the scenes you don't understand or to note parts of the scenes that strike you. If you have difficulty with some of Shakespeare's language, look at an annotated copy of *Hamlet* that provides explanations of difficult lines.

In these scenes, we are not concerned with the attitude of the author as we look at tone. Instead, we are interested in Hamlet's attitude and how it is revealed. In other words, the study of tone in these scenes is a study of how Shakespeare reveals Hamlet's attitude toward his situation and the other characters in the play.

Discuss:

1. In Act 2, scene 2, what is Hamlet's attitude toward
   * Denmark,
   * Rosencrantz and Guildenstern, and
   * his life in general?

   What is the tone in this scene?

2. In Act 3, scene 2, what is Hamlet's attitude toward
   * Gertrude,
   * his own problems, and
   * Rosencrantz and Guildenstern?

   What is the tone in this scene, and how is it different from the tone in Act 2, scene 2?

Apply:

Write a paragraph that expresses an attitude of disdain and disgust about a place. It can be a place you have been to or a place you have imagined. Don't explain your attitude; instead, reveal your attitude through vivid and precise use of language. Exchange your paragraph with a partner and see if you can correctly identify each other's tone.

Shakespeare: Lesson One

Consider:

HAMLET: Anything but to th' purpose. You were sent for, and there is a kind of confession in your looks which your modesties have not craft enough to color. I know the **good** king and queen have sent for you.

Discuss:

1. By Act 2, scene 2, we know that Hamlet does not think well of the king or the queen. Why does he call them *good*? How does this diction help set the tone of the scene?

2. How would it change the tone if Shakespeare had used one of the following words instead of *good*?
   * noble
   * corrupt
   * royal

Apply:

Write one or two sentences that express disdain for people who abuse their pets. Select words that reveal a sarcastic and bitterly critical tone. Share your sentences with the class.

Shakespeare: Lesson Two

Consider:

HAMLET: I have of late, but wherefore I know not, lost all my **mirth**, forgone all custom of exercises, and, indeed, it goes so heavily with my disposition that this goodly frame, the earth, seems to me a sterile promontory; this most excellent canopy, the air, look you, this brave o'er-hanging firmament, this majestical roof, fretted with golden fire—why, it appeareth nothing to me but a foul and pestilent congregation of vapors.

Discuss:

1. Hamlet complains that he has lost his *mirth*. How would it change the tone of the passage if he had said *happiness* or *goodwill* instead of *mirth*?

2. There are many perfect words in this speech, words that capture Hamlet's attitude toward his life and establish the tone. Select two words that perfectly set the tone, and be prepared to defend your choice in a class discussion.

Apply:

Rewrite Hamlet's speech in modern English, maintaining the same meaning and tone. Work with a partner to rewrite the speech and then share your results with the class. Pay particular attention to the words you choose.

Detail

Shakespeare: Lesson One

Consider:

HAMLET: Beggar that I am, I am even poor in thanks; but I thank you, and sure, dear friends, my thanks are too dear a halfpenny. Were you not sent for? Is it your own inclining? Is it a free visitation? Come, come, deal justly with me. Come, come; nay, speak.

GUILDENSTERN: What should we say, my lord?

HAMLET: Anything but to th' purpose. You were sent for, and there is a kind of confession in your looks which your modesties have not craft enough to color. I know the good king and queen have sent for you.

Discuss:

1. What details in this passage support Hamlet's declaration that Rosencrantz and Guildenstern were *sent for*?

2. What does the choice of detail reveal about Hamlet's attitude toward his friends?

Apply:

Write a conversation between two friends in dialogue. Friend number one has been bullying a younger student, and friend number two is angrily confronting him or her about it. Use detail to express and support friend number two's attitude toward friend number one. Share your conversation with a partner.

Shakespeare: Lesson Two

Consider:

What a piece of work is a man, how noble in reason, how infinite in faculties, in form and moving how express and admirable; in action how like an angel, in apprehension how like a god: the beauty of the world, the paragon of animals—and yet, to me, what is this quintessence of dust?

Discuss:

1. What details support Hamlet's assertion that man (meaning all people) is the *paragon of animals*?

2. Once Hamlet has established his view of the perfection of humans, he dismisses the *paragon of animals* by calling humans *this quintessence of dust*. What effect does the lack of detail to support Hamlet's dismissal have on the reader?

Apply:

Think about a book, movie, or video game most people you know have liked but you strongly disliked. Write a paragraph praising the book, movie, or game. Use at least three vivid details to support a general statement of its merit. Then write a single sentence that strongly and absolutely dismisses the positive evaluation. Use Shakespeare's words as a model. Share your work with the class.

Figurative Language

Shakespeare: Lesson One

Consider:

HAMLET: Sir, I cannot.

ROSENCRANTZ: What, my lord?

HAMLET: Make you a wholesome answer. My wit's diseased. But, sir, such answer as I can make, you shall command—or, rather, as you say, my mother. Therefore no more but to the matter. My mother, you say—

ROSENCRANTZ: Then thus she says: your behavior has struck her into amazement and admiration.

HAMLET: O wonderful son that can so 'stonish a mother! But is there no sequel at the heels of this mother's admiration? Impart.

Discuss:

1. Explain the use of irony in this passage.

2. How does the use of irony contribute to the tone of the passage?

Apply:

Rewrite the passage without the irony and discuss with a partner how the tone of the passage changes. It's fine to use modern English.

Figurative Language
Shakespeare: Lesson Two

Consider:

HAMLET: Why, look you now, how unworthy a thing you make of me! You would play upon me, you would seem to know my stops, you would pluck out the heart of my mystery, you would sound me from my lowest note to the top of my compass; and there is much music, excellent voice, in this little organ, yet cannot you make it speak. 'Sblood, do you think I am easier to be played on than a pipe? Call me what instrument you will, though you can fret me, you cannot play upon me.

Discuss:

1. Identify the extended metaphor in this passage and the literal and figurative terms.

2. What effect does the use of an extended metaphor have on the reader? Why do you think Shakespeare uses a metaphor rather than straightforward explanation to express tone?

Apply:

Write an extended metaphor that conveys an angry tone. Write about a time you confronted someone about cheating, the mistreatment of animals, or doing harm to the environment; or choose a topic of your own. Select your literal and figurative terms carefully. Share your metaphor with the class.

Shakespeare: Lesson One

Consider:

> *HAMLET:* Denmark's a prison.
>
> *ROSENCRANTZ:* Then is the world one.
>
> *HAMLET:* A goodly one, in which there are many confines, wards, and dungeons, Denmark being one o' th' worst.

Discuss:

1. Discuss the pictures that come to your mind when you read this passage. How do these visual images help the reader understand Hamlet's attitude toward Denmark?

2. The imagery in this passage is also figurative. Explain how the imagery and the figurative language work together to establish tone.

Apply:

Write a sentence or two that expresses your view of a place you do not like. Use imagery that is also figurative to reveal your attitude toward the place. Share your sentences with a partner.

Imagery

Shakespeare: Lesson Two

Consider:

HAMLET: . . . O, the recorders! Let me see one. [*He takes a recorder and turns to Guildenstern.*] . . . . Will you play upon this pipe?

GUILDENSTERN: My lord, I cannot.

HAMLET: I pray you.

GUILDENSTERN: Believe me, I cannot.

HAMLET: I do beseech you.

GUILDENSTERN: I know no touch of it, my lord.

HAMLET: It is as easy as lying. Govern these ventages with your fingers and thumb, give it breath with your mouth, and it will discourse most eloquent music. Look you, these are the stops.

Discuss:

1. What kind of imagery is used in this passage? Is it literal or figurative?

2. How does the imagery support the tone of the scene?

Apply:

Act out this scene with a partner. Emphasize the imagery of the passage with your tone of voice to convey Hamlet's attitude toward Rosencrantz and Guildenstern.

Syntax

Shakespeare: Lesson One

Consider:

> HAMLET: What news?
>
> ROSENCRANTZ: None, my lord, but that the world's grown honest.
>
> HAMLET: Then is doomsday near. But your news is not true. Let me question more in particular. What have you, my good friends, deserved at the hands of Fortune that she sends you to prison hither?
>
> GUILDENSTERN: Prison, my lord?
>
> HAMLET: Denmark's a prison.

Discuss:

1. When Hamlet says "*Then is doomsday near,*" he is not following the normal word order of English (subject, verb, complement). The normal word order would read like this: *Then doomsday is near*. How does this inversion of the normal word order affect the meaning of the lines?

2. What effect does sentence length have on the reader's understanding of this passage?

Apply:

Write a short, emphatic sentence to follow the long sentence below.

The Internet has become ubiquitous in our lives, providing information, connecting us with others, and filling our lives with a perplexing array of choices.

© 2000–2019 Instruction by Nancy Dean from *Voice Lessons*. This page may be reproduced for classroom use only.

174 | VOICE LESSONS

Syntax

Shakespeare: Lesson Two

Consider:

GUILDENSTERN: The Queen your mother, in most great affliction of spirit, hath sent me to you.

HAMLET: You are welcome.

GUILDENSTERN: Nay, good my lord, this courtesy is not of the right breed. If it shall please you to make me a wholesome answer, I will do your mother's commandment. If not, your pardon and my return shall be the end of my business.

HAMLET: Sir, I cannot.

ROSENCRANTZ: What, my lord?

HAMLET: Make you a wholesome answer. My wit's diseased.

Discuss:

1. How does Guildenstern's periodic sentence (*The Queen your mother, in most great affliction of spirit, hath sent me to you.*) help shape the tone of the passage?

2. Notice that Hamlet's replies in this passage are all short. How do these short replies help the reader understand Hamlet's attitude toward Rosencrantz and Guildenstern?

Apply:

Write a periodic sentence about being called to the office about an infraction you did not commit. Create a tone that is urgent and wary.

Tone

Shakespeare: Lesson Two

Consider:

Think about the tone of these two scenes from *Hamlet* and how Shakespeare uses the elements of voice to portray Hamlet's attitude toward his situation and the other characters. Now that you have looked more deeply into the way these scenes are crafted, answer the discussion questions again to see if your understanding of Hamlet's attitude and the tone of the scenes has changed.

Discuss:

1. In Act 2, scene 2, what is Hamlet's attitude toward
   * Denmark,
   * Rosencrantz and Guildenstern, and
   * his life in general?

   What is the tone in this scene?

2. In Act 3, scene 2, what is Hamlet's attitude toward
   * Gertrude,
   * his own problems, and
   * Rosencrantz and Guildenstern?

   What is the tone in this scene and how is it different from the tone in Act 2, scene 2?

Apply:

Write a brief essay analyzing the tone of either Act 2, scene 2 <u>or</u> Act 3, scene 2. Focus on <u>how</u> the tone is conveyed. Consider the elements of voice and how they shape the reader's understanding. Use textual support as evidence for your analysis.

Your Turn

Shakespeare: Culminating Lesson

Consider:

Think about the two scenes from *Hamlet* and how Shakespeare creates tone. Now write a scene from a play, an essay, or a poem of your own on the theme of betrayal. In your scene, essay, or poem, you will develop your own tone and express your own voice.

Discuss:

1. Identify the tone you want to create in your scene, essay, or poem.

2. How will you express your tone and voice using diction, detail, figurative language, imagery, and syntax?

Apply:

Write a scene from a play, an essay, or a poem of your own on the topic of betrayal. Approach it any way you like, but be consistent and clear. Be certain you use all of the elements of voice to shape your tone and express your voice.

Discussion Suggestions
William Shakespeare, *Hamlet*

Tone: Lesson One

1. I have split the tone lessons so that students can see how a close analysis of a difficult text improves their grasp of both tone and voice. Tone: Lesson Two repeats the questions of Lesson One to see how students have grown in understanding of the ways authors build tone and express voice. This question stresses the importance of Hamlet's attitude as a determiner of tone and voice. In discussing this question with students, I suggest that you accept all answers and write them on a chart without judgment. You can then compare their answers after students have experienced the lessons about the other elements of voice.

2. This question also addresses Hamlet's attitude toward his situation and the other characters. It is this attitude that sets the tone for the scene. Again, in this lesson, I suggest that you accept all answers and write them on a chart without judgment. You can then compare answers after students have experienced the lessons about the other elements of voice.

Diction: Lesson One

1. Hamlet is in a vortex of confusion, despair, and hesitation. How does he carry out his father's dreadful command? Is he mad? Does he feign madness? How does he even talk to his friends? Calling the king and queen *good* accomplishes several purposes. He can test Rosencrantz and Guildenstern's loyalty (to him or to the king?); he can throw his friends off guard and exact a confession that they were

called for; he can send a disguised message of scorn. The reader (or viewer) knows that the king is far from *good*, so the word is also used ironically, allowing the reader (or viewer) in on the sarcasm implicit in the word. The diction here thus sets a tone of ambiguity, manipulation, and bitterness.

2. If Shakespeare had used the word *noble*, the tone would be much less ambiguous and bitter. Although it could still possibly be sarcasm, the tone moves more into the realm of praise than criticism. If Hamlet had called the king and queen *corrupt*, the tone would be direct and critical. *Royal* has no evaluative connotations, and the tone would be more neutral. It will be interesting to hear students' views on these words. The important focus of the question is the importance of words in shaping and determining tone.

Diction: Lesson Two

1. The word *mirth* implies laughter and fun. There is a carefree feeling about the word. *Happiness* implies contentment and pleasure; *goodwill* implies compassion and understanding. Changing diction changes tone. The tone would change from the sadness of lost merriment to the regret of lost serenity to the isolation of lost consideration. Words have power to create tone.

2. Students have many words to choose from: *goodly frame, the earth*; *sterile promontory*; *most excellent canopy, the air*; *brave o'er-hanging firmament*; **majestical roof, fretted with golden fire**; **foul and pestilent congregation of vapors**. The contrast in

diction between how Hamlet formerly viewed the world and how he sees it now shows his bleak attitude toward his life and sets a tone of misery and despair.

Detail: Lesson One

1. Hamlet's first speech is filled with questions imploring his friends to tell the truth, implying that they were, indeed, sent for. Then, in his second speech, Hamlet recognizes their guilty looks (*there is a kind of confession in your looks which your modesties have not craft enough to color*) confirming his suspicions.

2. The detail in this passage sets up Hamlet's mistrust of Rosencrantz and Guildenstern and his disdain for their lack of loyalty to him. The details also show how easily Hamlet manipulates his old friends, who turn out to be disloyal sycophants rather than friends. Although there is a hint of a compliment when he tells them their *modesties have not craft enough to color* their assignment from the king, Hamlet remains mistrustful and contemptuous of them both.

Detail: Lesson Two

1. Details include statements that people are
   - *noble in reason* (honorable in thinking)
   - *infinite in faculties* (possessed of countless abilities)
   - *in form and moving how express and admirable* (graceful and worthy of praise)
   - *in action how like an angel* (able to do great good)
   - *the beauty of the world* (the highest form of life)

2. By reducing people to the *quintessence of dust*, Hamlet negates all of the admirable qualities he has established. People are dust, nothing more. The lack of detail gives the negativity of the statement precision and power. Had Shakespeare gone on and on about how Hamlet hates the world and the people in it, the speech would have degenerated into pathos and self-pity. Instead, Shakespeare gives us the unembellished, raw truth of Hamlet's despondency.

Figurative Language: Lesson One

1. The irony in this passage can be found in the final four lines. It is based on word play, which allows Hamlet to say one thing and mean another. His mother says that Hamlet's behavior *has struck her into amazement and admiration*. What she means is that Hamlet's behavior has astonished and shocked her. Hamlet twists her words to his own purpose and replies, *O wonderful son that can so 'stonish a mother!* He intentionally changes the meaning of the word *astonish* from the negative connotation (shock and outrage) to the positive (wonder and admiration) by calling himself a *wonderful son*. And he refers to his mother's *admiration* as though it were positive, which it most definitely is not.

2. The use of irony reinforces the bitter, angry, and sarcastic tone of the passage. Here Hamlet turns his anger on both Rosencrantz and his mother. His anger is controlled and delivered through irony and innuendo, but it is still there, shaping the tone of the scene.

Figurative Language: Lesson Two

1. The extended metaphor on the simplest level is the comparison between Hamlet and the recorder. The literal term is Hamlet and the figurative term is the recorder. But as Hamlet extends and develops the metaphor, we understand its deeper meaning. Guildenstern's (and, by implication, Rosencrantz's—they are interchangeable) unsuccessful attempt to manipulate Hamlet into a confession is compared to Guildenstern's inability to play the recorder. The musical imagery in the speech details the comparison, ending with a final pun: *though you can fret me, you cannot play upon me.* Fret (usually applied to a stringed instrument) refers to divisions of an instrument that help with finger placement, but it also means to trouble or annoy. Here the word means both. Hamlet refuses to be played.

2. The extended metaphor gives the reader insight into Hamlet's character and helps us to understand the mistrust and anger that underpin the tone. It also makes readers sympathetic to Hamlet's cause. Even his old friends have betrayed him. The metaphor works better than straightforward explanation because it brings the reader (or viewer) into the immediacy of the scene. We can hear the anger in his voice; we can see him push the recorder into Guildenstern's hand; we can understand every aspect of the comparison. The metaphor makes the betrayal concrete, clear, and appalling.

Imagery: Lesson One

1. Students may have a variety of answers for this question. But most will mention a dark prison with a labyrinthine hall and lots of cells. One of the darkest and most horrible of the cells is Denmark. The visual images clearly disclose Hamlet's attitude toward Denmark as a dark and threatening place, one where Hamlet is forced to be against his inclinations.

2. The image is also a metaphor, with *Denmark* the literal term and *the worst of all prison cells* the figurative term. The image sets up the mood: dark, threatening, and hopeless. The metaphor sets up the comparison. The reader has a picture of a prison, and the metaphor connects the image to Denmark and the tone of despair that surrounds Hamlet.

Imagery: Lesson Two

1. The imagery in this passage is visual (the characters see the recorder); tactile (Guildenstern knows *no touch of it*, Hamlet tells Guildenstern to *Govern these ventages with your fingers and thumb*); and auditory (*it will discourse most eloquent music*). The imagery is literal. The only part of this passage that is figurative is the simile, *It [playing the recorder] is as easy as lying*, and the simile does not express an image.

2. The tone of the scene centers around Hamlet's attitude toward Rosencrantz and Guildenstern. Hamlet taunts them, evades their questions, and misleads them. The tone is thus bitter, sarcastic, angry, and mocking. The imagery in this passage supports the tone by showing Hamlet in action: mocking and manipulating his visitors.

Syntax: Lesson One

1. The inversion of normal word order shifts the focus of the sentence. Both versions of the sentence have the same fundamental meaning, but the unusual word order brings out the connection between Rosencrantz's contention that *the world's grown honest* and Hamlet's refutation. It becomes an *if . . . then* statement: If the world has grown honest (and is in its current state), then the end of the world is near. The word order also emphasizes the word *doomsday* by placing it in an unusual position.

2. The short sentences deliver Hamlet's zingers. He asks his visitors, *"What news?"* knowing that they will lie. He negates their comment that *the world's grown honest* with *Then is doomsday near.* He declares *Denmark's a prison* without elaboration. Through Hamlet's short, sharp sentences, the reader understands that Hamlet is in control of the conversation and can shift it as he wishes. Rosencrantz and Guildenstern are left confused and floundering.

Syntax: Lesson Two

1. Periodic sentences create high tension and interest: The reader (or listener) must wait until the end of the sentence to understand the meaning. Here the periodic sentence builds a sense of urgency. The distraught queen has sent Guildenstern to fetch Hamlet. By leaving the most important part of the message to the end, the sentence builds the tone of distress. She has sent for Hamlet, and we know Hamlet will not respond agreeably.

2. Hamlet's short replies have two functions. First, they present Rosencrantz and Guildenstern with the possibility that Hamlet may be mad (his inappropriate reply, *You are welcome*, and his statement that his *wit's diseased*), a stance certain to mislead his visitors. Second, the short sentences create an abrupt dismissal of Rosencrantz and Guildenstern. Hamlet cannot be bothered with a long reply to his duplicitous friends. Indeed, he protests that he cannot make *a wholesome answer*. Rosencrantz and Guildenstern hold no interest for Hamlet; they are a nuisance to be brushed off.

Tone: Lesson Two

1. I have split the tone lessons so that students can see how a close analysis of a complex text improves their grasp of both tone and voice. This lesson repeats the questions of Tone: Lesson One to see how students have grown in understanding of the ways authors build tone and express voice. This question stresses the importance of Hamlet's attitude as a determiner of tone and voice. In Act 2, scene 2, Hamlet's attitude toward Denmark, Rosencrantz and Guildenstern, and his life in general is dark and troubled. He calls Denmark a *prison*; he taunts and manipulates Rosencrantz and Guildenstern; he views the people around him as *this quintessence of dust*. Yet the tone in this scene is not universally negative. Although he taunts Rosencrantz and Guildenstern, there is something almost playful about the way he manipulates them. He also earnestly solicits the truth and gets it. And in the end of the scene, he reveals his misery (although not the cause) to his old friends. The tone is more one of sadness and confusion than anger. Any variation of these answers is acceptable as long as students support their answers with evidence from the text. As students discuss these questions again, take notes on a large chart. Compare this chart with

the chart you developed with students at the beginning of this section. Lead a discussion about the ways close analysis of a piece of writing deepens with knowledge of the elements of voice.

2. This question also addresses Hamlet's attitude toward his situation and the other characters, and it is this attitude that sets the tone for the scene. In Act 3, scene 2, Hamlet is much more angry, bitter, and sarcastic. He pretends to misunderstand his mother's *amazement*; he misleads Rosencrantz and Guildenstern; he taunts Guildenstern with the recorder. The tone is heated, disillusioned, and troubled. Gone is any sense of playfulness or hope for support from his friends. It is a pivotal scene in Hamlet's attitude and the play's tone. Students may express different answers to these questions. Their answers are acceptable, of course, if they can support their answers with evidence from the text. As in Question 1, take notes on a chart while students discuss these questions. Compare this chart with the one you developed with students at the beginning of this section. Lead a discussion about the ways close analysis of a piece of writing deepens with knowledge of the elements of voice.

Your Turn: Culminating Lesson

1. If students have trouble deciding on a way to develop the theme, it would be helpful to take some time to guide them (by modeling, brainstorming, graphic organizers, freewriting) to find a compelling topic, narrow their approach, and gather ideas. It would also be helpful to give students quiet time to think and then time to discuss ideas in pairs or small groups. Ultimately, students will have to decide on their own theme and how they will develop it; but support and guidance never hurt. What they decide will determine their tone and help shape their voice. Students should jot down their topic and some ideas about development to keep in mind as they draft their plays, essays, or poems.

2. Students will also have to decide the tone they want to develop in their work. By now they should understand that they have the power to craft a specific tone through focused use of the elements of voice. If they keep a specific tone in mind, they will shape their writing in such a way as to reveal their tone to their readers. Voice is individual and distinctive. Will their writings be passionate? Cool and brassy? Balanced and rational? Sarcastic? Angry? Hopeful? Ironic? For this assignment, students should have the freedom to develop their own voices through the skillful use of the elements of voice.

Bibliography

Austen, Jane. *Sense and Sensibility*. London: Macmillan and Co., 1902.

Bacon, Francis. "Of Studies," *The Essays or Counsels, Civil and Moral*. London: A. Swalle and T. Childe, 1696.

Blake, William. "My Pretty Rose Tree," *Songs of Experience*. London: R. Brimley Johnson, 1901.

Boswell, James. *Boswell's London Journal 1762–1763*. F. A. Pottle (Ed.). New York: McGraw-Hill, 1950.

Brontë, Emily. *Wuthering Heights*. London: Chesterfield Society, 1900.

Browning, Robert. "Childe Roland to the Dark Tower Came," *A Victorian Anthology, 1837–1896*. E. C. Stedman (Ed.). Cambridge: Houghton Mifflin, 1895.

Chopin, Kate. *The Awakening*. Chicago: H. S. Stone, 1899.

Coleridge, Samuel Taylor. *Biographia Literaria*. London: G. Bell and Sons, 1891.

Coleridge, Samuel Taylor. "The Rime of the Ancient Mariner." New York: D. Appleton & Co., 1857.

Conrad, Joseph. "The Lagoon." *Cornhill Magazine*, January 1897.

Conrad, Joseph. *Lord Jim*. New York: New American Library, 1920.

Donne, John. "Death Be Not Proud," *The Poems of John Donne*. Oxford: Clarendon Press, 1912.

Douglass, Frederick. "Letter to My Old Master, Thomas Auld," *My Bondage and My Freedom*. New York: Miller, Orton & Mulligan, 1855.

Eliot, George. *Silas Marner*. London: William Blackwood and Sons, 1861.

Frost, Robert. "The Death of the Hired Man," *North of Boston*. New York: H. Holt and Co., 1914.

Hardy, Thomas. *The Mayor of Casterbridge: A Story of a Man of Character*. London: Sampson Low, Marston Searle, and Rivington, 1887.

Hazlitt, William. "On Going a Journey," *Table Talk: Essays on Men and Manners*. London: Bell & Daldy, 1871.

Joyce, James. "The Dead," *Dubliners*. London: Grant Richards, 1914.

Joyce, James. "I Hear an Army," *Selections from Modern Poets*. London: Martin Secker, 1921.

Kennedy, John F. Inaugural Address (January 20, 1961), Presidential Speeches, Miller Center, UVA.

Kennedy, John F. Remarks at Amherst College (October 26, 1963), John F. Kennedy Presidential Library and Museum, Columbia Point, Boston, MA.

Lawrence, D. H. "The Horse-Dealer's Daughter," *England, My England, and Other Stories*. New York: Thomas Seltzer, 1922.

Macaulay, Thomas Babington. *Life of Samuel Johnson*. Boston: Ginn and Co., 1903.

Mansfield, Katherine. "A Dill Pickle," *Bliss and Other Stories*. London: Constable, 1920.

Milton, John. *Paradise Lost*, Book VI. London: Samuel Simmons, 1667.

Pope, Alexander. "An Essay on Man." *Pope's The Rape of the Lock and Other Poems*. T. M. Parrott (Ed.). Boston: Ginn & Co., 1906.

Red Jacket, Chief. "Indian Speech, Delivered Before a Gentleman Missionary, from Massachusetts, by a Chief, Commonly Called by the White People Red Jacket. His Indian Name Is Sagu-ya-what-hath, Which Being Interpreted, Is Keeper-Awake," Speech to the U.S. Senate by Red Jacket. Boston: Nathaniel Coverly, 1805.

Roosevelt, Franklin Delano. First Inaugural Address (March 12, 1933), Presidential Speeches, Miller Center, UVA.

Schopenhauer, Arthur. "On Noise," *The Essays of Schopenhauer*. London: G. Bell and Sons, 1891.

Shakespeare, William. *Hamlet, The Works of Shakespeare*, Vol. 8. Stratford-on-Avon, England: The Shakespeare Head Press, 1904.

Shakespeare, William. *Macbeth, The Works of Shakespeare*, Vol. 8. Stratford-on-Avon, England: The Shakespeare Head Press, 1904.

Shakespeare, William. Sonnet 116, *The Works of Shakespeare*, Vol. 10. Stratford-on-Avon, England: The Shakespeare Head Press, 1907.

Swift, Jonathan. "A Modest Proposal." Dublin: S. Harding, 1729.

Thoreau, Henry David. *Walden*. Boston: Ticknor and Fields, 1854.

Twain, Mark. "Fenimore Cooper's Further Literary Offences," *New England Quarterly*. Bernard DeVoto (Ed.). Greenwich, CT: Fawcett Publications, 1946.

Whitman, Walt. "Song of Myself," *Leaves of Grass*. Brooklyn: Self-published, 1855.

Wilde, Oscar. *The Importance of Being Earnest*. Premiered in London, 1895.

Wilson, Woodrow. Address to Congress Requesting a Declaration of War Against Germany (April 2, 1917), Presidential Speeches, Miller Center, UVA.

Yeats, W. B. "The Song of Wandering Aengus," *The Wind Among the Reeds*. London: Elkin Mathews, 1899.

Maupin House
capstone

At Maupin House by Capstone Professional, we continue to look for professional development resources that support grades K–12 classroom teachers in areas, such as these:

Literacy	Language Arts
Content-Area Literacy	Research-Based Practices
Assessment	Inquiry
Technology	Differentiation
Standards-Based Instruction	School Safety
Classroom Management	School Community

If you have an idea for a professional development resource, visit our Become an Author website at:

http://www.capstonepub.com/classroom/
professional-development/become-an-author/

———————————————

There are two ways to submit questions and proposals.

You may send them electronically to:
proposals@capstonepd.com

You may send them via postal mail. Please be sure to include a self-addressed stamped envelope for us to return materials.

Acquisitions Editor
Capstone Professional
1710 Roe Crest Drive
North Mankato, MN 56003